ISBN-13 978-981-94-5590-4 (Digital/Kindle)
ISBN-13 978-981-94-5589-8 (Hardback)
ISBN-13 978-981-94-5631-4 (Paperback)

Archive Photos (Approval Pending)

20090000069 - 0002 - F W York Collection, courtesy of National Archives of Singapore
19980005081 - 0087 - Courtesy of National Archives of Singapore
19980001166 - 0109 - Ministry of Information and the Arts Collection, courtesy of National Archives of Singapore

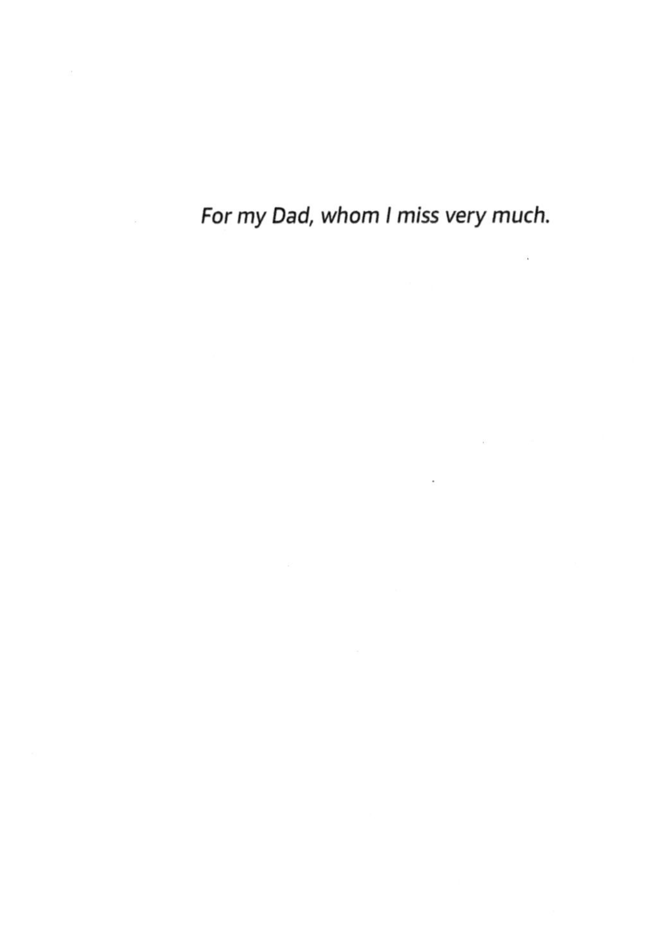

For my Dad, whom I miss very much.

CONTENTS

Copyright
Dedication
Everybody Wants To Rule The World 1
Preface 2
Part I 3
1- The Five-Note Jingle 4
2 - The Six Mile 8
3 - A Place Without Fear 17
4 - What Normal Looks Like 23
5 - The Broken Pencil Case 28
6 - The Price of Safety 33
7 - Power That Isn't Bought 39
8 - Three Joss Sticks 44
9 - What Effort Looks Like 49
10 - Between Two Worlds 55
11 - You Spin Me Like A Record 61
11 - Becoming 66

12 - The Thing She Doesn't Ask Twice 71
13 - Let Sleeping Dogs Lie 77
14 - The Price of Power 81
15 - The Quiet Shift 85
Part II 94
16 - Four Minutes of Light 95
17 - The Long Way Out 100
18 - The Centre of Gravity 106
19 - The Measure of a Life 111
20 - What He Thinks He's Protecting 117
21 - Don't Do Anything Stupid 123
22 - The Stairwell 126
23 - The Cost of Being Defended 132
24 - The Quiet After 137
Part III 141
25 - Activation 142
26 - What Wasn't Said 147
27 - Quiet Intervention 152
28 - Doing Nothing Wasn't Neutral 157
29 - Everything Falls Apart 164
30 - Leadership Without Exposure 171
31 - Acting on Your Best Behaviour 175
32 - When the Rain Passed 179
33 - Learning to Stay 184

34 - What Power Costs 188
Epilogue 196
From The Author 199
Archive Photos 201

EVERYBODY WANTS TO RULE THE WORLD

What If You Were Part Of The
Very Thing You Avoided

PREFACE

Set in rural 1980s Singapore, this literary memoir follows a quiet, introspective boy coming of age in a working-class neighbourhood as he searches for belonging in the spaces between faith, friendship, and fear. Drawn first to the safety of church life and a tender, unspoken bond with a girl named Trish, he later drifts toward a secret society whose promise of protection offers an escape from bullying and powerlessness at school.

As violence edges closer and loyalties fracture, he is forced to confront the cost of silence, the limits of passive survival, and the quiet authority of a father he has long misunderstood. Moving between innocence and moral compromise, the story traces how restraint, chance, and small acts of intervention shape a life—and how real power is not found in dominance, but in the courage to step away before it is too late.

PART I

1- THE FIVE-NOTE JINGLE

THE sun was bright this morning, its warmth pressing through the windscreen as the car moved easily along the highway. Traffic was especially light that day, for some reason. The radio was belting 80s hits, making it especially pleasant and nostalgic. To me, music has always been more than just a pleasant tune. It was a marker of the different stages in my life, a reminder of a milestone or a significant point, a memory.

The little five note jingle at the start of the song, followed by a subtle chorus of synthesizer tunes and its shuffle groove that was so distinct that anyone who listens to it will know the song. *Everybody Wants To Rule The World* from *Tears For Fears* was playing and I knew every word of this song.

Written during the Cold War, the song captures an innate, often insatiable human desire for power, control, and influence. To me, it conveyed mixed feelings of loss, and a hopeful future. Maybe it wasn't the lyrics of the song itself, but it was the music and how it lifted me emotionally with its powerful drum beat.

I haven't heard this song in a while. But listening to the song now as an adult reminded me of a moment in time. As the first few lines of the song drew me in, I tightened, my heart skipped a beat. Some memories don't announce themselves; they wait for the right sound.

"Welcome to your life, there's no turning back."

The words triggered a memory and a panic. My heart raced. It reminded me of tension and release. Growing up in a conservative Catholic environment. But it wasn't conservative—it was far from it.

As the car moved forward, steady and untroubled, I meandered through vehicles effortlessly. The scene felt familiar to me. Many years ago, I had taken a similar route, on many bus rides along the same road growing up. I would day dream about the uncertain future.

Unconsciously, as the memories of the past hit me one by one, my right foot felt heavier and heavier on the accelerator pedal. The car sped up, swerving left and right. I found myself gripping the steering wheel tighter.

The traffic light in the distance had turned red. In a split second, I had to decide whether to beat it or to stop. To speed up or slow down.

I slowed and stopped at the traffic light and a deep breath followed.

My mind wandered to a memory that has long stayed with me. A meeting that one night that I would never forget, in a dark corner of the wet market that I once disliked.

Stepping into the market, the smell of dead fish and pork sold during the day lingered in the air. The wet floor and little drains of water around each stall that still had remnants of blood and guts. As I walked, I could hear the sounds of my shoes, sploshing on the puddles of murky water on the ground.

It always made me uncomfortable walking through it. I had a feeling of disgust and nausea as I went deeper and deeper into the maze of hawker stores, criss crossing each other. The canvas that covered the stores created a kaleidoscope of olive green and dark grey shades, making the walk more ominous and uneasy.

As I came to an opening, the path became brighter, the ceiling lit with some hanging incandescent bulbs. I saw some people sitting sparsely over wooden tables, drinking warm bottled beer. The tone was hushed and whispers were predominant.

I was 16, turning 17.

A deep voice. "Aren't you someone that is good

at studies? Don't come back, ever. Go and live your life."

All I can remember now is that those words echoed throughout the rest of my life. No drama or significant event. After I heard those words, my heart pounded loudly inside of me. As meekly as possible, I nodded, drew my wooden chair from where I sat, making as little sound as possible, stood up with minimal eye contact and walked away slowly and quietly without looking behind.

I wasn't sure if I was released or dismissed at that time. But I was determined to move away from that reality.

I heard a small beep of a car horn behind and was jolted back to the present. The light had turned green and was still waiting to drive off. Another beep.

Embarrassed, I waved my hand in apology. I stepped on the gas pedal and sped off.

I realised I had also moved on with my life. A few stops, a few beeps, and then, forward and onward.

***

2 - THE SIX MILE

GROWING up in the 70s and 80s, I was a small-framed, skinny, bespectacled boy. I was a little goofy and spent much of my time riding my rusty bicycle around the neighbourhood. At that time, the area was still taking shape, with newly built government flats rising around my home.

Down the road was a wet market that sold fresh seafood and meat from open stalls. We called it Six Mile, simply because it sat at the sixth mile marker along the long road that stretched from the city. It was the only wet market for miles, long before supermarkets were introduced, and it was always bustling—especially on weekend mornings.

When I was old enough to receive a daily allowance from my parents, I sometimes skipped lunch after school so I could save enough money to buy the latest album on cassette tape at the end of the month. My favourite pastime was spending hours after school at a small music shop at the corner of the bus interchange, browsing shelves stacked with cassette tapes.

"Just browsing or are you going to buy today?" the music shop owner asked, from behind his counter.

He recognised me as a regular.

"Not sure, Uncle," I replied.

"Anything new?"

My wallet was especially thin that day.

"Shipment didn't come today," he said, sounding a little disappointed.

"But I have the last piece of the new album from *Tears For Fears*. Want? Very popular," as he reached under the counter and showed me the black and white cover of the cassette tape—*Songs From The Big Chair*.

I looked at it carefully, in its plastic shrink wrap, turning it over and looking at the song titles. I have their previous album, *The Hurting*, and it was really good. Reaching into my pocket, I sighed. I gave him my last five dollars. No lunch for me today.

My brothers were much older and spent most of their time in Secondary school or out with friends. Still, they were my earliest influence when it came to music. They brought home vinyl—7 and 12-inch singles and albums—and I learned how to create my own mixtapes using recordable cassettes. We had an old vinyl record player with red and white output jacks, hooked up to a stereo system with a cassette deck that could record.

"Press that red button—the one that has the circle on it," my brother said.

"Don't forget the Pause button, the equal sign."

"Okay, now put the needle on the record."

It took some getting used to. Sometimes the needle would jump and ruin the entire recording. Sometimes, I released the pause button too slowly and the first parts of the song were not recorded. But once I mastered the sequence, it was addictive. That was the world I escaped into.

My life also revolved around the neighbourhood Catholic church. It was an old, Gothic-style building with a tall grey spire, built in the late 1800s, and it stood next to my school, which was also Catholic. The church and school sat at the seventh mile, at the end of the same road where Six Mile market was located.

Early in the morning, the church bells would ring—twice, followed by the muted opening tone of the church organ, calling the neighbourhood to prayer. It was the start of the Morning Mass—the beginning of the day for some parishioners who woke up early and made their way to church. The entire neighbourhood was mostly Catholic and Masses were held in both English and Chinese Dialect.

On each side of the main road, the area was filled

with small dirt paths leading to other paths—sprawling with zinc roofed huts and coconut trees. Some grounds were larger than others, where small animals like chickens, pigs and goats were kept. Neighbours were friendly and gossip was plenty, passed from one hut to the next.

There was a jetty near school where fishermen would bring their catch of the day, early in the morning and sell them at Six Mile. Sometimes, I would wander into the jetty early in the morning and would catch a glimpse of the boats arriving at the jetty, with the fishermen rolling their nets and sorting their catch.

"Boy, come closer. Look at my catch," the fisherman would say, as he tilted his basket.

But I would only nod my head and return a forced smile.

It was fun to watch them, but I didn't like the smell of the ocean, or the stench of seafood and kept my distance from the boats. Perched at the nearest dock, I would look intently. I loved how they would unload and organise things as they came to shore. Baskets of fish would be unloaded and sorted. I would watch for a few moments—but only from afar.

"Next time, uncle," I replied and gave a quick wave.

There was a small bus depot at the end of the road. Only two bus routes would end their journey there. Transportation in and out of the neighbourhood was through these two buses. They were hot, sweaty and rattled loudly as we rode in them. For ten cents, we could take that bus route into town. They were crowded all the time and often, there was only standing space. Every inch of that bus ride was maximised. As young children, we would squeeze into every crack that was available as the bus moved.

Opposite the school was a small row of attap-roofed shophouses where we bought *rojak,* which was a fruit salad mixed with dark prawn paste and coloured sugared drinks. Totally unhealthy, but definitely delicious. And the combination hit the spot every time.

I had attended that school since Primary One. It wasn't far from my home—only a few bus stops away. My parents didn't want to send me to the same school as my brothers, who were downtown. They were pragmatic about it. And from Primary Three, my dad taught me how to take the bus to school every morning.

My early childhood memories were of catching small guppies in nearby streams after school, buying glass marbles, stickers, and plastic animals, or *kuti-kuti* as we called them, from the drinks vendor —treasures we used in recess-time games—before grabbing an ice lolly and heading home. Life was simple then.

When I turned thirteen, I joined the church's altar boys' society. The Mass on Sundays intrigued me as a young boy—the vestments and the rituals. I wanted to experience it first hand. And so I learned the rituals up close and how to assist the priest during Mass. There was the genuflect, the kneeling and the pouring of water and altar wine for the priest that made it a sombre and sacred service. We had dawned white cassocks, very much like the priests, but wore sashes around our waist, instead of chasubles. Putting our outstretched hands together above our chest, we also synchronised our bows together with the priest. It showed reverence and respect at the same time, as the congregation bowed back. This was my favourite gesture and I loved it.

In the early 1980s, a global recession affected Singapore. Many people lost their livelihoods. My father was not spared; he eventually lost his well-paying corporate job. My mother, determined to put food on the table, rented a small shop downtown and started a business selling women's clothing. For a while, my father stayed home watching television, until the end of 1985, when he joined my mother at the shop—managing customers while she handled alterations and sold made-to-measure clothes.

"Here's five dollars for the week. Don't spend it all on *kuti-kuti*," said my father, as they left for the shop in the morning.

"I don't," I protested.

But the fact was that I had been losing at the schoolyard games. I needed more practice flipping those plastic animals over my opponents.

They were gone most of the time, tending to the business. I was mostly left to my own devices. That was when the house became quieter.

Because of my size—and my lack of confidence—bigger boys at school picked on me constantly. It was just part of life: school bags ripped apart, belongings going missing. You learned not to complain, only to avoid certain people. We attended an all-boys neighbourhood school. It was a constant power struggle between the weak and the strong. Each class had nearly fifty students, and the teachers struggled to manage both education and the daily chaos. Often, they simply chose not to intervene.

Our principal was a hardline disciplinarian. From time to time, he would line up one or two students for public caning—usually for theft or street fighting. His famous line was "Choose one," spoken as he gestured toward a cabinet of canes of different sizes. These punishments, however, did little to stop what happened beyond school grounds. Outside, a different code ruled—street justice enforced by informal gangs that shaped school life.

I remember one incident vividly. I had bought a

new pair of clean white shoes from the market the day before. As I got off a public bus after school, I was shoved aside and cornered by four or five boys from another class.

"Somebody has new shoes today," said one of the boys.

"Let me go," I protested and started to walk away.

But the bigger boys blocked me.

"Let's see if these shoes are good," said another.

They grabbed my arms and carried me to the back of the bus stop. Indignant, I didn't make a sound or protest. There wasn't a need to. I only knew the inevitable and wanted it to pass quickly.

One by one, they took turns stomping on my shoes until they were filthy. Their actions were quick—it barely hurt. But they left me there, humiliated and shaken.

I learned early what it meant to remain invisible.

That was when being active in church began to make sense. It was an escape from bullying inside school and the dangers outside it. I wanted somewhere safe, somewhere those boys wouldn't follow.

Ironically, I wasn't particularly pious. As an altar boy, I served the Masses I was assigned to each week. I also volunteered for early morning weekday services because the older boys didn't want to wake up so early, and I filled in occasionally on Sundays. But since most of the altar boys came from the same school, I often found myself trapped in the same social hierarchies and bullying dynamics. It was the Sunday Catechism classes that offered some relief from the constant vigilance of my daily life.

Thirteen was the age when Catholic children attended Sunday Catechism classes in preparation for Confirmation. I was enrolled in the church's programme and attended these classes. It was considered the norm for a young child to be Confirmed by the age of 14. It was a two year programme that everyone had to attend. It was held at the Church Centre, which was an extension of the church and down the road. So every Sunday, we would form a small line and make our way to the Church Centre after morning Mass.

Sunday classes were mixed-gender. Even then, the boys sat on one side of the room and the girls on the other. We were awkward, unsure of ourselves. Still, children from all over the neighbourhood attended. For the first time, I was meeting people outside my school. I don't remember the names of anyone from my Catechism class now. But during church camps—held twice a year during school holidays—we formed new cliques and friendships.

It was at one of those camps that I met Tricia.

***

3 - A PLACE WITHOUT FEAR

CHURCH camp was held twice a year. It would start on a Friday evening and end on Sunday late afternoon. It was one of the things I looked forward to all year. I would pack for the weekend into a small nylon duffel bag and walk to the church centre which was just further down the road from where I lived.

Each time before camp, I felt a sense of anticipation—of doing something fun, something out of the ordinary, and of meeting friends. It was my escape for the weekend. And when it ended, I always felt a little lost, drained of energy—missing my friends and already yearning for the next one.

Growing up Catholic meant certain traditions and customs had to be followed. As a child, you were expected to be Confirmed, and the only way to do that was through Sunday classes. The kids who turned up for camp didn't have much choice. They were told to attend, and there they were. We weren't exactly filled with joy in the light of Christ, nor particularly spiritual or prayerful. But for me, it was different. I really liked it for a very different reason. I cherished the experience of being with my friends.

It gave me a sense of belonging outside of school —where I wasn't bullied and didn't have to live with fear. I met kids who weren't rough. There was a sense of security.

I hadn't really noticed anyone during my first camp in the initial year. I was timid and didn't reach out to anyone. It was also my first time away from home and everything was so new to me.

But during the next camp, I noticed a girl from another class who stood out. She was unusually tanned, darker than most, and taller than me. She had small eyes behind black-rimmed glasses and wore her hair in a long ponytail. She was often hovering around a group of girls from her school.

Perhaps it was the way she carried herself, the sound of her voice—deeper than most—or her quiet self-awareness that drew my attention. I immediately wanted to meet her, but I was too shy to say hello. I had very little self-esteem then. I felt invisible, like I looked like everyone else, never speaking up during camp sessions. Still, whenever I could, I would steal a glance in her direction.

If our eyes met, I would straighten my posture instinctively and look away almost immediately. Sometimes she seemed to notice my awkwardness and smiled to herself. When she smiled, she lit up the room. It felt like everyone smiled with her. I found comfort just watching her during sessions, noticing how she interacted with the facilitator—often answering questions with poise and confidence.

Her name was Tricia.

At that camp, I also met someone who was just as awkward as I was—Michael. He was from a different school and was much bigger than me, almost a head taller, but we shared a love for music. Because of that, we quickly became inseparable. One night, as we talked about bands we liked, we discovered that we both loved *Tears For Fears* and their recently released album *Songs from the Big Chair*. Our favourite song from the album? *Everybody Wants To Rule The World*. The song had peaked at number one on the US Billboard Charts.

Together, we memorised every word and sang it constantly whenever we were together. After camp, we met before and after Sunday school, talking nonstop about new songs climbing the charts. It was something that we bonded over.

As teenagers growing up in the 80s, birthday parties or dance parties—affectionately called "functions"—were common. A host would invite a group of friends, who would then invite others, often resulting in gatecrashers filling the house. This was socially acceptable back then. There was no alcohol, but there was plenty of music, dancing, and excitement—*Depeche Mode, Wham*, and others blaring from speakers.

Some parties had rotating coloured lights and spinning mirror balls. When a spotlight hit them, reflections scattered across the room, filling the space with moving points of light. It was all the rage, and we looked forward to it.

Through Michael, I was invited to far more parties than I ever would have been otherwise. Occasionally, I would bump into Tricia and her schoolmates. Whenever I saw her, I froze at the back of the dance floor. I stayed quiet, awkward, and said nothing. But she always knew I was there. She would glance at me from the corner of her eye and smile.

Finally, at a 1985 Christmas party, I found the courage to approach her.

"You're Alan, right?" she said, amid the loud music, before I could say anything.

"Erm, yeah," I replied, unsure of myself.

"Tricia. But you can call me Trish."

That was when we officially became friends. She called me "`Lan."

That Christmas party included a gift exchange. Each person brought a small, inexpensive gift and placed it into a shared pool. Anyone who contributed could take one in return. The gifts were unmarked and anonymous—it added to the excitement of the exchange.

In anticipation, I looked at the pile. Nothing caught my eye, except an unusual one that was in a brown paper wrapping. Some of the others were in gold trimmings and neatly held together with paper ribbons. But strangely, this one stood out and I picked it up and examined it. Neatly wrapped, it was the size of a box of chocolates, but was narrow and long. It felt light and metallic. I shook it, expecting to hear it rumble, but there wasn't a sound. Unwrapping the edges to take a peek, it was matte black with rounded edges and something metal and cold.

Trish walked over.

"I hope you like the pencil case," she said as she disappeared into the crowd.

The following January, I brought a pencil case to school. The night before, I transferred all my stationery to it, neatly tucking everything. Everything found a place—just like it should.

It didn't last two days.

Another boy in my class stabbed the cover repeatedly with a pen and then stomped on it until it was ruined.

Devastated, I went home, wrapped the broken pencil case in an old newspaper, and threw it away quietly. I never told Trish what happened.

***

4 - WHAT NORMAL LOOKS LIKE

MICHAEL was taller than me by a head, a little on the pudgy side but had a shuffle to his walk that made him unmatched. He reminds me of John Travolta in the opening scene of Saturday Night Fever, strutting across New York city to the beat of Bee Gees. You could imagine him, slightly hunched, with his headphones worn on his neck, high-fiving everyone that came along, and seamlessly weaving through school corridors without fuss. And because he was medium built, he wasn't a push over. Few would lay a hand on him without being shoved back. But he was a gentle soul and blended quickly into any circle of friends. If you looked at him in a crowd, you might miss him. He looked like everybody else. He could get along with people, given his easy going nature.

We bonded over music quickly. My interests for music outside of the mainstream also appealed similarly to him. He was a walking encyclopedia of artists, lyrics and different beats. He would spend hours listening to a track over and over, picking up subtleties in tone or pitch. He would track the charts each week and introduce them to me.

Besides music, and tracking the Billboard 100 religiously, he was a nerd and loved to read just about anything and everything. He knew stuff about things that you never knew about and could spend hours going into detail. Teachers loved him —he wasn't at the top of the class, but he turned in his homework, was respectful to teachers and classmates. I once asked him why he wasn't the top student in class, and his reply made sense.

"Being at the top is too much pressure. I'd rather be behind and no one will have any expectations of me."

It wasn't that he wasn't bullied. The bullies stayed away from him because he knew how to push back. Besides, he knew how to talk his way out of anything. When he sensed that there was something going on, negotiations would generally solve his problems. Sometimes he would have some Snicker bars in his bag and give them freely out. Bribery kept the rougher kids at bay. He bought security another way.

Michael knew enough not to get into people's affairs. He was a keen observer of human behaviour, so to speak. His favourite motto was "Let sleeping dogs lie". Sometimes, if he felt strongly about something, it wasn't in his nature to do something about it. He would just observe the situation more, sit on it and let it play out. As long as no one was hurt in the process, he would just shrug and be on his way. He would feel sick when he saw someone smaller being bullied in school. But he never intervened to protect the weak. He knew the consequences of intervention and he wanted to stay away from trouble. If he did, there would be retaliation and he didn't want that. He wanted peace.

He was allowed to go about his business, had no major issues with anyone, and wasn't too interested in relationships at that age. It wasn't that he didn't like anyone. He would have crushes like any normal teenager. But he would never rock the friendship boat. He feared that once he confessed to a girl that he liked her, it was all over. The friendship wouldn't last and they would never talk again. Perhaps it was his defense mechanism that kicked in.

To me, Michael was the symbol of normal. That's what I liked about him. Hanging with him made me feel normal. In a world of tension, fear and bullies, being with him was safe. He was my buffer and safety net. He was easy to get along with and we could talk for hours about simply everything and nothing. Conversations could drift from one topic to another with ease and no awkward silences.

"Did you know that there is a counter rhythm in *Everybody Wants To Rule The World*? Here, listen carefully."

That was how most conversations would start, with something that he had recently discovered, or a fun fact.

"Oh, yeah," I would always respond and just listen to him rattle on.

Over time, I would learn ways to say something silly in response to him and go back and forth.

We went everywhere together at church. We're like Earth and the Moon. We would be seen in each other's orbit. If someone was looking for Michael, they would ask me and vice versa. We weren't joined to the hip, and inseparable. But sooner or later, we would gravitate towards each other.

It wasn't that he was popular either. He wasn't tall, dark or handsome. But people generally wanted him around. It would be awkward to have something on and not invite Michael. If I was invited for something, it was common knowledge that Michael would go with me. And so, during those days, we did many things together. He was my wingman—with him by my side, I wouldn't feel insecure.

The strangest thing was I never knew much about his parents. I knew his younger brother from church. Despite our closeness, I was never invited to his home to hang out and he never came to mine.

***

5 - THE BROKEN PENCIL CASE

I knew who destroyed the metal pencil case Trish had given me.

He was a new boy, recently transferred to the school and placed in my class. He wasn't much taller than me and sat a few rows back. From the first day he joined, he seemed to have a thing for me. He didn't say much, but whenever he had the chance, he taunted me. I tried to avoid him, but somehow he always found his way to me. Along the corridors, he would bump into my shoulder. On the stairs, he tried to trip me. During recess, he would drag his hand across my desk and spill whatever I was eating. I hated him, but I couldn't resist.

He often hung around a group of three other boys who were also recalcitrant and regularly broke school rules. They came late to school and, instead of reporting to the General Office, sneaked in through the back gate, jumped the fence, and hid in the toilets until morning assembly was over. Then they would casually join the rest of us as we made our way to class.

He was a lazy student and rarely took notes during lessons. Instead, he harassed others for theirs. Once, he was caught cheating during a class test, leaning over to copy his neighbour's answers. Teachers noticed his behaviour but did very little to stop it.

Every Monday, we had Physical Education or P.E. We changed into our school shorts and T-shirts and went outdoors for stretching, jogging, or relay sprints. It broke the monotony of classroom lessons and was something most of us looked forward to after the weekend. He, however, usually stayed behind, finding excuses to avoid P.E.. He hated physical activity, and everyone knew it. As a result, no one ever included him in interclass sports.

On Monday, I brought my new metal pencil case to school. It was P.E. day. We all left the classroom —except him. He claimed to have a stomach ache and asked to be excused, as he often did. So he stayed behind. During moments like this, he took the opportunity to rifle through other students' belongings, steal notes, or copy homework.

When I returned to class, I noticed small dents on my pencil case. Tiny poke marks on the cover. It was new. How could this have happened? I wondered if I had dropped it or knocked it onto the floor. I suspected it was him, but I had no proof. In those days, you didn't go to your form-teacher over things like this. You accepted reality and learned to be more careful.

The next day, after recess, I returned to find the pencil case completely ruined. It was riddled with poke marks and flattened almost beyond recognition. My pens, pencils, and correction fluid were broken. White fluid had spilled everywhere inside. It was destroyed.

I asked around quietly. A classmate told me he had been seen in class during recess. He had used my pen to stab the case repeatedly, then dropped it onto the floor and stomped on it. I looked under his desk and glanced at his shoes. There were traces of correction fluid on the soles.

After school, I overheard him bragging to his friends. He said it felt good poking holes into my pencil case. The more he did it, the better it felt. He laughed and said it looked too good for someone like me—that I deserved a broken one.

I noticed later that people already knew before I told anyone.

I was furious. Of everything he had done, this felt like the worst. And because the pencil case came from Trish, it cut deeper. I was powerless against him. It was mindless fun for him, but it felt like a real loss to me.

The thought of payback haunted me. But all I could imagine was being hit or kicked. I was smaller. I was no match for him physically. Still, I wanted revenge.

So I hatched a plan for the following week's P.E. session. I would fake an illness and stay behind. That would be my chance—to search his bag and destroy his things the way he destroyed mine. I had never done anything like this before. But the rage inside me felt unbearable. If there were no consequences for him, I needed some for myself.

"Teacher, I sprained my ankle last night," I told the P.E. teacher.

"Okay, you stay in class—the rest of you, go to the school yard now."

It was a common excuse that we used quite effectively at the time. It couldn't be diagnosed, didn't require the nurse, and it meant staying in class. Everyone left for P.E., including him. I waited until the room was empty, then moved quickly. I opened his bag, emptied its contents, tore pages from his books, and stomped on a few of his belongings before stuffing everything back inside.

As I returned to my seat, he suddenly walked in.

My heart raced. I froze. He had faked an injury again. He went to his desk, opened his bag, and immediately knew what had happened. He was furious.

"You!" he shouted and pointed at me.

In a split second, without a word, he turned and hurled his chair at me.

I ducked.

It missed me by inches.

I ran.

I hid in an empty toilet cubicle and locked myself in until P.E. was over. I waited and waited, sweat rolling down my forehead and into my shirt. When the bell rang, I waited until I could hear the shuffling of feet in the hallways. As the sounds of footsteps became weaker and weaker, I returned to class.

His chair was back in place. The next teacher was already there. I sat down, shaking, barely able to focus.

When school ended, I ran straight to the bus stop. I was afraid he and his friends would follow me. If they caught me, I knew what was coming.

That night, I didn't catch much sleep. Tossing and turning, one thought circled endlessly in my head: How could I make this stop?

I will see him again tomorrow. And I had no protection.

***

6 - THE PRICE OF SAFETY

MIDWAY through my first year of Sunday class, a new group of boys joined us. They were from the same school as Michael but from another class. They dressed differently and carried themselves more confidently.

I got to know them quickly through Michael. They moved like a pack of wolves—scanning, observing and circling. One didn't go anywhere without the other. It didn't matter to be much at the time. Most kids hung around in groups. They all lived outside my neighbourhood, and it was a change for me. I quickly found myself drawn to them.

I grew especially close to one of them—Victor—whose father was a physician and whose mother was a nurse. They lived in an affluent neighbourhood with well-kept houses. He was different from the other guys and dressed in the latest fashion —Giordano jeans and Fila collared tees. He was clearly from a well-to-do family and held himself that way. He was outspoken and confident, joking constantly and making sarcastic remarks that drew laughter from the others. But he also had a dark nature and would talk about the destruction of the world, World War III and how defenceless Singapore would be if war broke out with our neighbours. Although I found him questionable at times, I thought he was just being candid and spoke his mind.

Soon enough, I would spend my after-school days at one of their homes. There was a sense of safety there—real safety—not just comfort. We weren't out on the streets hanging around in public places like MacDonald's or downtown shopping centres like Far East Plaza. We were at home, hanging around and doing our things.

Occasionally, we went to the nearby Study Room at the Community Centre, or to the Country Club that Victor's family belonged to. Through him, I met other kids from other schools. It didn't take me long to realize there was a life beyond the one I knew at my own school. It was a fresh change for me as I had the opportunity to meet people around my age, outside of school and outside of church.

Sometimes I stayed at Victor's place to study. My studies had been declining, as I struggled to focus on anything outside of Church. Each semester, my results worsened, and my parents became increasingly worried that I was mixing with the wrong company. I would meet them for dinner with sullen looks, missing belongings, or dirty school uniforms. It was a relief to them that I now had decent company, and so they readily allowed me to sleep over.

Victor was an aspiring DJ, and pocket money was never a concern. His parents were higher income earners, and he could afford all the vinyl records, mixing decks, and stereo equipment he wanted. I was drawn to him by our shared love of music and the ease of his friendship. We went to functions together—sometimes he was paid to DJ, other times he volunteered his services for free. He taught me how to count beats of the music, analyse song transitions and which was the best time to release the next song to match the beats. I immersed myself into that world and wanted to learn more.

I hadn't lost my closeness to Michael. We still met regularly during Sunday class. But now, there was a life filling the space between Church and school. Besides listening to music, we shared little else. He was studious and was either studying or reading his favourite novel of the week. I was poor in my studies and wasn't into much reading. But with Victor, I was drawing deeper into the world of music and that got me excited. My mixtapes were getting more interesting as the songs that I chose were matching rhythm and beats.

One night, while studying at Victor's home, I opened up to him about my struggles in school—

the bullying, the pencil case incident and the constant fear of showing up each day. At first, he shrugged it off and teased me, which only made me feel worse.

"Why not join a gang? We'll make sure you don't get beaten up—ever," he said casually, as the conversation deepened.

"Wait—who is 'we'," I asked.

He revealed that the group I had been spending time with was part of a neighbourhood gang that held weekly meetings around the Six Mile wet market. Victor assured me the commitment was minimal—just showing up once a week. That alone, he said, would deter school bullies. But if anyone in the gang needed help, we were expected to stand together.

"Oh," I replied.

"So does that make you a..."

He didn't respond. He just looked down and continued looking at his textbook. And then I understood.

I was conflicted. I never wanted to be part of the very thing I had spent my teenage years avoiding. My life had been shaped by escape—not by the idea that if you couldn't beat them, you should join them. Here I was, finally feeling safe in a healthy environment, only to find myself back where I started—on the verge of gang life again.

At night, scenarios started playing in my head. If I drew power from this association, I would be left alone in school. No one would dare touch my belongings. I could eat during recess uninterrupted. I could take the bus home without being followed or shoved.

I realised I was already thinking about it as if it were settled.

I searched my feelings and wondered if this was something I wanted to do. Frankly, I was uneasy. I felt that it was against my principles as a Catholic. I was not keen on violence and secret societies because it was against the law and I could potentially be wrapped up in violence and all kinds of illegal activities. But somehow, Victor normalised it. He made it like it was no big deal—that it was normal for kids to be part of it. And besides, Victor's guys were part of it, so we wouldn't be alone in it. There was safety in numbers and we could rely on each other for help. It would be a "safer" group that we would be joining and no one would know this. We would only agree to do "certain" things and not others. We could decide.

The price of safety was association—membership. It was also being physically available at all times when they called. This also meant loyalty and secrecy. I wasn't sure I was ready for it. It was too fast and too soon for me.

"I can't stand this indecision. Married with a lack of

vision,"

I felt the song was mocking me.

For the next few days, I avoided Victor and the others, trying to sort through my thoughts. I spent days thinking about the consequences—about betraying my own beliefs and about what it meant to give in. I wondered whether I was weak-minded, or simply a product of my circumstances. With them, I could have safety. Without them, I would return to fear.

Was this a way out for me?

***

7 - POWER THAT ISN'T BOUGHT

VICTOR learnt independence and welded control over others at a young age. His parents worked in the hospital. They were gone many odd hours of the day—sometimes early in the morning or night shifts. They were on call 24/7 and their hours were not predictable. His father was a pediatric gynaecologist and his mother worked as the head nurse of a major local hospital. The two had met in the maternity ward and fell in love. They had married later in age, than most couples at that time and Victor was their favourite mistake. They had time for only one child—Victor and did their best to make him comfortable.

And so, he was brought up by the family helper, who was with the family since the very beginning of his life. She attended to all his needs as a child, but never replaced the authority his parents outsourced. He learnt to ask and he received everything that he needed. He never experienced any major hardship or challenges in life. His helper would feed him his meals up until about 10 or 11 years old and shuttled him by taxi to and from after-school classes, everything from poetry, music to art.

As an only child, he had a dedicated playroom in the house where in the younger years, was filled with the best toys and was gradually replaced with a piano, electric guitars, stereo systems, direct drive record players and sound mixing consoles. The items would be upgraded as his interests upgraded.

Victor's circle of friends was small. From young, he would only hang out with a group of friends that were children of their parent's friends. And nothing more. Although he was popular in school —many kids loved to admire the things that he would bring to school, like the newest Nintendo Game Boy, he chose his inner circle carefully. His parents taught him to be very selective about everything that he bought. It had to be the highest quality otherwise they would break easily. It was the same philosophy about friends. He would choose them carefully, otherwise they would fail him. These friends were incredibly loyal to him and would do anything for each other.

As a person who had everything served to him and everything that money could buy, going to a public school, which his parents insisted, was a way of making him normal. School uniforms, standard canvas shoes and white socks was the rule. He could not wear anything outside it. This made him feel a little disappointed that he couldn't wear expensive shoes or a nice cotton shirt (school uniforms were all polyester). But there were no rules outside these few items to wear. So he wore a nice Tag Heuer Sports watch, and his accessories and school bag was that of a popular Japanese brand [ixi:z]. He would often carry the latest Sony Walkmans, buy the latest vinyl records and so on.

He didn't care too much about studies either. There was no pressure to perform well in school. At a young age, he knew that eventually everything his family owned would be his. His slog would not be the same as everyone else. He would not have to pursue a corporate career like most kids. He wouldn't have to make money like everyone else.

But he realized his big pocket money could not buy power and influence in school. The rougher kids would just laugh him off as a rich spoilt kid. He wasn't small and so he wasn't picked on too much. They knew his parents were well-to-do, and hence they had the impression that he was well connected and not to mess around too much with him. But he didn't have power and their respect.

So he decided to taste power. He was the first to get involved with the Six Mile neighbourhood society by befriending a rougher kid with tattoos.

He was intrigued that the rougher kid was able to command the respect of the others around him. He was the go-to guy, if there was a street problem. He had ink images of the Monkey God on his chest or the Taoist God of War on his entire back. Victor was envious of those gang colours. It demonstrated a freedom he never had with his parents.

He did hint to his parents once that he wanted tattoos, but was firmly rejected.

"Are you a gangster?" his father would say.

"No—getting a tattoo doesn't mean I'm one," he shot back.

But he did it anyway. Discreetly, he inked a dragon on the inside of his right shoulder so that it would not be noticed. He believed it marked him—that it meant something now followed him. Eventually, he joined them as a member because it was a natural progression for him. It was his path to power and gaining respect.

He was a keen student of gang life. He loved the rituals, the quiet respect that they accorded one another, and the secret hand gestures that they passed to one another on the street to recognise each other. He was very conversant with the street rules and how they were important in the way of "outside" life, beyond school. He was aware of the rules of engagement between groups and navigated it whenever there was a street challenge between rival gangs.

But most of all, he loved the hierarchy—the elders, the seniors and the core members. He was told the easiest way to level up was to recruit. And the first people he recruited were his immediate circle of friends. They created their own sub-rules, inner culture and decided how they would organise themselves and what they would get involved with and what they avoided. Their loyalty to each other ensured that they operated as one, with Victor as their de facto leader.

Through that, Victor was able to consolidate power, weld influence that money could not buy and control more people as he grew up.

Someone had suggested to him that the church was a great way to recruit members. His parents were non-practicing Catholics, and had no deep ties with church. But when Victor suggested he wants to be Confirmed, they were surprised. As everything in his life, whatever he wanted, he did. And so, he and his friends found themselves at Confirmation Class, checking the scene out.

***

8 - THREE JOSS STICKS

AFTER several weeks of pondering over it and keeping my distance from Victor and his guys—eventually, I caved.

"Okay, I'll do it," I told Victor.

"Do what?" he asked.

"Join the gang."

I missed the music mixing, the functions and the camaraderie we had built, and I couldn't move past my loneliness or my need to belong somewhere. This need was stronger than any clandestine activities that I may be part of. At this point, I was unaware of any. I was naïve enough to believe this was a more "normalised" version of things. After all, we were just kids. We promised that we would not get into racketeering or extortion activities, but stick to personal protection for our own advantage. And so, like any new recruit, I went with Victor and the others to the Six Mile market one evening to meet the seniors.

I dreaded walking into the market, much less at night. It had a large zinc roof that covered the market. Some parts had canvas covers. It had a stench that was distinctive of rusty metal, damp canvas and rotting seafood. The floors were always wet, and you had to walk gingerly across the grime. It unsettled me. Whenever my parents went to the market over the weekend, I would always make some excuse and avoid going. It was a place that I found little joy in visiting. I wanted to leave as soon as I arrived.

Tonight, I told myself I would get used to it. This was another price that I had to pay for association—being comfortable with the uncomfortable. As a teenager, I had many strong convictions about many things—my sense of duty, difference between right and wrong, and of authority and justice. My Catholic faith reinforced this. That night, those pillars were shaken—one by one.

As we arrived at the meeting place deep into the dimly lit market, I saw a few people seated sparsely on broken tables and chairs. Some tables had empty beer bottles, with red-faced occupants. I noticed that they had been drinking for a while before we got there. It wasn't a late night drinking party. This felt different. There was no loud conversation, laughter or music. It was tense and measured. Voices were hushed as matters were discussed and decisions made.

The seniors sat at one table—many of whom I recognised from church or school. I was surprised to see how many people I had known for years at the venue. It was unnerving. I never knew they were part of this.

Some took a quick look at me and went back to their discussion, unbothered. Some glared at us, but left us alone. I felt very uncomfortable and unwelcomed at first, but before the night was over, I told myself I had to either state my intention and purpose for being there, or risk being threatened at school, or worse. I was already seen and could expose what was going on.

We chose a table and sat ourselves down. To blend in, we had a few bottles of beer on the table, but neither of us drank from the cups except Victor. I guess he wanted to look cool, like a senior. It appeared to me that Victor and the guys were considered new or insignificant—they didn't have too many conversations with the seniors. We mostly kept to ourselves all night, showing presence but not too much for fear of offending the seniors.

One of the seniors I recognized came to our table and started talking to us. He was from another class in my school, a few levels higher, in Secondary Five. They were the rougher kids. The ones that had delayed graduation, some for more than a couple of years, due to poorer grades. After they have reached the limits of when they could stay in school, they would either drop out or go to a vocational institute to learn a trade. This senior was almost 18 this year, with tattoos on his arms and legs.

Victor introduced us. He was the one recruiting him. The senior took one look at me and scoffed, and questioned my value to the gang. It was clear I wanted protection.

"Hey shorty, why do you want to join us?" he asked, half mocking me. Victor gestured to him and whispered something to his ear.

It was straightforward. As long as part of my pocket money found its way into his wallet, I could have all the affiliation I wanted. That was all he was interested in. Money in exchange for power. This was another price to pay for power. He talked about loyalty and street justice and the need to protect our "brothers" all the time. He was the leader of our area and all matters of concern would go to him.

As the night came to an end, I pledged allegiance at a Taoist altar set up at the back of an alley, my friends standing as witnesses. I was a Catholic altar boy, kneeling with three joss sticks in my hands, bowing to a Taoist god I did not believe in.

I was now part of the Six Mile neighbourhood gang.

Ironically, I felt almost mechanical—emptied of emotion. I was stunned by how things had unravelled. I had gone to Church to escape gang life, only to end up part of one. As I knelt there, the lyrics of *Everybody Wants To Rule The World* played in my mind again—only now, the song carried a different meaning. Power.

I went home with mixed feelings that night. There was no relief, no exhilaration. I had done something that I felt was unnerving, and felt extremely conflicted.

***

9 - WHAT EFFORT LOOKS LIKE

MY dad was raised Catholic and also attended Catholic school. He was baptised as an infant. As far as he was concerned, the Church was the end-all and be-all. It held the moral authority of the entire family and defined his decisions in life.

He was a man of few words. He believed that actions spoke louder than words, and as far as possible, he chose to show rather than explain. He didn't hug or kiss us. Instead, he showed us that strength of character and quiet confidence mattered more than bragging or showing off.

He came from a pioneer generation where most of his peers had only completed Primary School. He, however, had passed three GCE 'O' level subjects and was considered better educated than most. Yet he never acted superior. My mother was drawn to his quiet disposition and stability. He was a strong provider with a steady job in the private sector. Over the years, he stayed with one company from the very beginning, rose through the ranks, and eventually became its General Manager.

He never reminded us of his qualifications. He didn't need to. The way he carried himself made it clear what effort looked like. But he was adamant about one thing—education was the gateway to success. He made sure we went to school and reminded us, often without words, to take it seriously.

During the 1980s, a global economic recession spiralled out of control, and many people lost their jobs. These were difficult times, especially for the private sector. I had little recollection of the wider world then. All I knew was that more people were losing work, factories were closing, and everyone spoke about tightening their belts. We did too. We stopped eating out and cooked more at home. Shopping trips and movies were cut, and the only entertainment we could afford was free-to-air television.

My allowance was never reduced, but I consciously bought fewer cassette tapes from the local store. It would have felt insensitive to spend freely, even if I didn't fully understand the hardship around us.

The first time I realised my dad had been laid off was when he suddenly stayed home instead of going to work. It was strange seeing him without his dark trousers, long-sleeved shirt, and tie. He wore shorts and a white singlet, cleaning the house in the morning and preparing lunch before we returned from school. In the afternoons, he repaired broken items or tended to overgrown plants. In the evenings, he cooked dinner.

"Boy, take out the plates and lay the table," he would say.

His meals were simple—just cooked rice and a dish of stir fried vegetables and maybe some chicken. I wondered sometimes if he had a cookbook that he kept somewhere. He was able to whip out meals from thin air.

At first, I wasn't used to the fact that he was the homemaker now. Now, it was awkward to see him clear the plates and wash the dishes after dinner.

"Just leave it there," he pointed at the sink.

"I'll wash it."

My dad had never taken personal time off throughout his career. He often said he enjoyed work so much that he couldn't imagine staying away from it. Seeing him at home every day felt unnatural. It was June 1985 when his company was wound up. He was given three months to close its branches in Indonesia and Hong Kong—before laying himself off. At 45, he was considered too old for re-employment.

My mum was a homemaker, but to fill her

time, she began selling ready-made dresses to friends and neighbours, offering free alterations with each purchase. With the little money we had, she bought a sewing machine. Sometimes after dinner, I could hear the soft hum, mixed with a rhythmic clicking, whirring, or clacking as the machine's needle went up and down as she worked into the night, finishing orders. Business improved, and at her supplier's encouragement, she rented half a small shop downtown. By the second year, she had expanded to take over the entire shop.

The clothes she sold were inexpensive. Sometimes she bought used clothes, repaired and resold them. During the recession, her business remained largely unaffected. Her customers stayed loyal, and she weathered the storm. Seeing my father retrenched broke her heart. He was a proud man, and when it happened, he retreated into his sanctuary—our home—and rarely left it.

There was tension at first, perhaps even resentment. The family dynamics had shifted. My mother became the sole breadwinner, and an extended silence settled over us.

"Why don't you help me at the shop?" she asked my father.

"It's not much, but I could use some help," she continued.

"Let me think about it?" he replied.

"I have a job interview next week."

He had searched for work, responding to the increasingly thin employment ads in the local newspaper. But the job offers never came and it hurt his morale. Perhaps it was never meant to be.

By the end of 1985, my father finally joined my mom at the shop. Initially, he hesitated, believing he was overqualified. Eventually, he swallowed his pride and agreed, attending to customers while my mother focused on alterations. Later, as the economy recovered, they pivoted toward made-to-measure clothing.

Together, they built a successful small business —one that neither could have managed alone. They argued, like all couples do, but they shared a singular determination: we would stay together, never go hungry, and always have a roof over our heads.

Running a small business was exhausting. They worked from morning until late at night, including public holidays. I was convinced that without my father's organisation and planning skills, and my mother's sewing craft, they would not have succeeded. They adapted to change without fear—but that change came at a cost.

"Here's five dollars for the week. Don't spend it all on cassettes," said my father, as they left for the shop in the morning.

I never responded to him when he said that.

At a young age, I was left to fend for myself. When I got home from school, the house was empty. I learned to fill the hours alone. Homework was sometimes neglected as my days became filled with phone calls—first to Trish, later to Victor and the guys. I was given a daily allowance for lunch and often ate late dinners with my parents after they closed the shop at nine each night.

***

10 - BETWEEN TWO WORLDS

MY friendship with Trish had evolved into something deeper after we became friends following the Christmas party. Sometimes during the day, I would call her from my home phone, and we would talk for hours about anything and everything.

"Do you find Physics harder or Chemistry harder?" she asked.

"I don't know—but I don't like my Physics teacher. I can't understand anything he says," I replied.

"Maybe I'm just dumb."

"No, you're not—you just have a bad teacher."

We'll laugh at the silliest of things and comment about friends too.

"Michael is so weird—he asked me about my horoscope the other day," she said.

"And what did you say?" I asked her.

"Apart from the fact that we're Catholics and don't believe in horoscopes?"

Laughter followed. Conversations were easy and free flowing, never tense or pretentious.

She had two younger sisters and was the eldest in her family. Her father was a taxi driver who owned his own cab, and her mother was a homemaker. They came from a simple, humble background.

In many ways, her family circumstances drove her to be the best version of herself every day. That was precisely what drew me to her—she was pragmatic, self-driven, and confident.

Her group of friends was small, mostly from her school club—St John's Ambulance Brigade, or St. John's as she would call it. They were always together, during and after school. Her life revolved around club activities and competitions at the district levels. Every day, they practised. Their discipline and commitment bound and pushed them forward.

Our relationship was complicated. We were young, and as we grew closer, we were careful not to appear attached or to be seen as dating. Neither of us had ever been in an exclusive relationship. In those early days, the bond was felt but never acknowledged. We knew there would be rejection from our families if things became explicit. It was a time when boy-girl relationships were frowned upon until much later.

And so, we settled on calling each other "brother" and "sister." It allowed us to stay close without openly declaring a relationship to our friends. For the most part, it worked.

We organised group outings with church friends, and sometimes with members of her school club. We would go to East Coast Park, hire bicycles, and cycle for hours before ending the day at McDonald's. It was a way to spend time together without the awkwardness of a couple's date.

When we heard about a new movie involving time travel in a car—Back to the Future—we were eager to watch it. We organised a group outing with church friends and went downtown. Sitting next to her in the dark, sharing popcorn, our arms and shoulders occasionally brushing, felt innocent and electric in its own quiet way.

Michael was always part of these outings. I insisted on it. He was my constant companion then —my wingman. He kept me from feeling insecure. Whenever I ran out of things to say, I gravitated toward him. We would exchange silly observations about clothes, shoes, or anything around us.

This part of my life was pure and innocent. Being in those group settings helped me grow more confident around the opposite sex, but more importantly, it taught me what companionship felt like.

We had little money, but the pleasure of being together was enough.

I kept Victor and his group out of this world. Even though they knew each other, I instinctively tried to separate these parts of my life. Victor's influence was very different from Trish's group dynamic. He was more mature, wealthier, and surrounded by sophistication. He had everything a young person could dream of—a new BMX bicycle, high-end stereo equipment, and the latest vinyls, including 12-inch extended remixes. He showed me the ins and outs of mixing music live, something that was impossible for other kids our age. We simply did not have the means or access to the equipment.

Materially, he embodied everything a young person desired but couldn't have. Being an only child, perhaps he wished his parents were more present in his life. Their lives revolved around the hospital, and he was often alone. They compensated by giving him money and freedom.

Yet there was darkness to him. For someone who had everything, the one thing he lacked was power. And to obtain it, he turned to societal affiliations. It made him feel strong and influential. His friends were loyal to him—something money could not buy. Between these two worlds, I found that kind of power intoxicating. It was power without having to speak or explain yourself.

Over time, fissures formed between the two groups, and without realising it, I began to withdraw from Trish and her friends. I didn't want worlds colliding. It wasn't about class or money, I told myself. Unknowingly, it was about power—those who had it and those who didn't. I began to feel that Trish and her friends didn't wield the kind of influence that Victor did. As twisted as it sounds, this hunger for power pulled me further into darkness.

Trish noticed the change before I did. She sensed my withdrawal and my absence from Sunday classes.

"Hey, I missed you from Sunday class today," she said, one night she called.

"Yeah, I had a few things to do," I replied. I didn't. I just didn't feel like going that day.

"`Lan—is everything okay?"

"School work's been piling up and my parents want me to do some stuff. I'm fine. I'll see you next week?"

I lied. She knew something was wrong.

Our conversations grew heavier. I became more critical, more suspicious of people's motives. Our worlds had also grown apart. She would talk more about her club activities and competitions, while I spoke about functions and music and how to mix dance songs live. Neither of us was interested in the other. Sometimes we would fall into long silences, unsure of what to say. After a while, we would hang up, leaving things unresolved.

Once, she mentioned that her club was teaming up with Michael's school for competitions. As club captain, she was spending more time with the other school's captain—a new guy she had just met.

"So, there's this guy that's the captain," she told me one night.

"We're preparing for the district competition. I guess I'll be seeing him more," she continued, and then paused.

The moment she said it, my insecurity surfaced. My tone changed.

"Well, good luck with everything," I replied, sounding a bit sarcastic and insecure.

"Thanks," she replied, but it wasn't sincere. It was a brush off.

I grew quieter.

But as *brother* and *sister*, there was no space for confrontation. No permission for jealousy or argument. Only a fragile hope that this new friendship of hers wouldn't become something more.

In my mind, that was the beginning of the end.

***

11 - YOU SPIN ME LIKE A RECORD

FUNCTIONS were a part of growing up in the 80s. The people, the gate-crashing, the spinning lights, the mirror balls and the music. During the school holidays, we would get invitations to functions at least twice a week. My circle of friends had increased dramatically after hanging out with Victor. I wasn't sure what he saw in me that made him want to have me as part of his inner circle. Maybe he wanted a lackey to run around and do things for him. Maybe he just wanted to show his parents that he was capable of making new friends. Whatever the reason, I can't say that I did not benefit from associating myself with him. Through him, I learnt a lot about music and how it moved people.

Victor was obsessed with the latest DJ equipment and over time, he had amassed quite a bit of peripherals. When he was starting up, he rented his equipment from a local dealer. Over time, he thought he could have better control if he actually owned them. Money was no object—he would slowly build up a complete set of record players, mixers, speakers and lighting.

It was Victor that first introduced me to direct drive record players. They were special record players that didn't have an internal belt and could be used for stopping and releasing records. They could also speed up the tempo of the music through a slider. He would label each record based on beats per minute. That way, it was easier to match the beats of two songs by increasing the tempo of one to synchronise with the beats of the other. We would spend hours just practising mixing at his home.

He was invited to endless functions, which he called "gigs". Some of it was paid—he would rent out his equipment for the night and throw in his services as a DJ. This suited him fine as he slowly fine-tuned his abilities.

I would tag along, pack his equipment and records for the functions and watch him do his thing as the night went on. He would plan the playlist set and play it according to his plan. Sometimes, when he went for a break, I would stand in for him.

There was one function I remember clearly, held in a large living room with furniture pushed hard against the walls, coloured lights sweeping across the ceiling in slow, hypnotic arcs. The room was packed. Sweat hung in the air. When Victor stepped back from the decks to take a breather, he nodded toward me—a small, casual gesture—and I moved in to keep the music going. I played safe tracks, nothing risky, nothing that would shift the mood too sharply.

But when he returned, he placed a hand lightly on my shoulder and waited, not impatiently, just expectant.

"Okay, watch this," he said and took over the console.

I stepped aside immediately. As soon as he entered, the energy in the room lifted, almost on cue. Cheers went up. Someone shouted his name. The same equipment, the same records—but now the attention belonged entirely to him.

I stood near the wall, watching the crowd respond, aware for the first time that what I offered was usefulness, not presence. I was necessary, but only until I wasn't.

He liked the fact that he was able to match the energy of the crowd, just by playing the right music. He could also bring their excitement up, or down at will. Familiar tunes or jingles at the start of a hit song would stir the crowd's emotions and he knew when to introduce them and when to fade them out. He didn't speak—he let the music speak for itself. Powerful beats and hypnotic rhythms drew people into the moment.

From these moments, I could totally understand

why Victor lived for these gigs. It played to his desire for control. Through music, he had a way of controlling the temperature of the crowd, taking them any direction that he wanted them to go. It suited the kind of power he preferred—quiet, unquestioned.

Over time, I learnt about how music influenced moods. A strong inspirational song could lift the spirits of those who were down. A sad, melancholic tune could remind someone of an emotional moment. And then there were the slow songs—the ones that cleared the floor almost instinctively, leaving only couples behind, swaying awkwardly at first, before settling into the quiet permission the music offered.

Most of those songs lasted about four minutes. Long enough for two people to stand close without it being questioned. Long enough for hands to find their place without explanation—one at the waist, one at the shoulder—close enough to feel breath, but not close enough to require courage. Four minutes where movement replaced conversation, where no one had to decide anything beyond staying still together until the song ended.

There were times when I imagined Trish in those moments—not dancing wildly, not drawing attention, but standing there with me while the lights dimmed and the room softened around us. In my opinion, slow dancing was always easy. No words. No declarations. Just four minutes where the distance between us disappeared without needing to be addressed.

Can four minutes save the world?

But the song would always end. The lights would come back up. I would later understand that four minutes was not enough to change anything if you never stepped onto the floor in the first place.

At the end of the night, we would pack everything up and quietly move everything back to his home. The crowd would thin out, the lights would be switched off, and the rooms would return to their ordinary shapes. Without saying another word, we would withdraw into the silence of the night.

And then, at the next function, we would do it all over again—the same crates, the same wires, the same routines—each night blurring into the next, until the repetition began to feel less like momentum and more like motion without direction, the needle tracing the same groove over and over, wearing it down even as the music played on.

***

11 - BECOMING

BEFORE long, it was year end again and another church camp was organised. When it was announced, I couldn't wait for it to happen. Trish, Michael and I are much more acquainted with one another after the last one and this one was going to be much more enjoyable and fun.

Again, I packed my trusty small nylon duffel bag with clothes and essentials, but this time, I also shoved a few cassette tapes and mixtapes that were my favorite, borrowed my brother's Walkman for the weekend, and a headphone splitter. It was a new gadget that I found in the thrift shop—you could use two headphones at a time. At night, when the lights were off, I planned to meet up with Trish and Michael and spend the night hanging out and listening to our favorite music together.

That Friday night, my walk from home to the church centre gathered speed as I couldn't wait to get there. There were many thoughts running in my head. There were recent changes in my life and somehow they all confused me. The holding of joss sticks—kneeling at the Six Mile market, the hot and cold relationship that I felt with Trish lately, and the pull towards Victor and his guys. I was hoping that this camp could at least resolve some unsaid tension between me and Trish.

I was also conflicted about my Catholic faith and I regretted my actions at the Six Mile market. I did not regret it for the protection that I had presumed it would give. I regretted that I had betrayed my religious beliefs. Inside of me, church camp would somehow also renew my convictions about faith and hopefully bring me back.

Church camp was organised over 2 days and 2 nights. There were group sessions where we could split up and have sharing sessions about the topics that were planned. It was meant to extend the lessons that we had gone over on Sunday classes, and reinforce those learning points. Every session had some self reflection and one by one, we would discuss our thoughts and feelings. I kept waiting for something to settle inside me during those sessions—some sense of certainty, some reassurance —but nothing did.

Being introverted, this was quite hard for me. I could write down my thoughts, but I wasn't comfortable sharing them. I envied Trish and Michael for the way they could easily express themselves. Possibly because they didn't have so many secrets that they were hiding. I would pen all my thoughts down and then realise that some of it would expose me and I would start redacting them. In the end, I was left with not much to say. I had filtered everything out.

We would sleep on mattresses in separate rooms, split by gender, on different floors. After the lights were out, we were expected to stay in our rooms but that seldom happened. Everyone would wander around and hang out till the next morning. By that time, the church centre's main entrance would be locked so everyone would remain in the grounds.

After the lights were switched off, Michael nudged me with his foot and tilted his head toward the door. Trish was already standing, barefoot, holding her slippers in one hand. I reached into my bag, pulled out the cassette tapes and the Walkman, and followed them quietly down the corridor.

We climbed the narrow stairs to the rooftop and slipped outside. The night air was cooler up there, carrying the faint smell of rain and concrete. We lay flat on our backs, staring at the sky. I threaded the tape into the Walkman and passed one earpiece to Trish and the other to Michael. The music was soft, barely louder than our breathing.

"Can anyone find the Big Dipper?" Michael asked, squinting upward.

"What's that?" Trish said, laughing softly. "Something you dip into a very big bowl?"

Michael groaned and started explaining, pointing vaguely at the sky. Trish interrupted him every few seconds, and soon we were all whispering and laughing, careful not to carry our voices too far. Eventually, Michael's words slowed. His breathing deepened. The tape hissed gently between songs.

“`Lan,” Trish said quietly. “Why are you so quiet today?”

I turned my head toward her. Her face was half-lit by the distant streetlights, familiar and unreadable at the same time.

“I didn't know what to say,” I whispered.

That wasn't true. I knew exactly what to say. I just didn't know how to survive saying it. She waited. I could feel it—not impatience, not pressure. Just space. The kind she had always given me.

“I'm going through a lot right now,” I said finally. “I'll tell you some other time. Okay?”

She nodded, accepting it without question. She didn't push. She never did. After a while, she turned, curled over to my side and fell asleep, her earphone still in place. I lay there listening to the tape click and rewind softly, watching the sky fade toward morning, knowing that something between us had shifted, quietly and without ceremony.

When I was sure she was asleep, I muttered something I hadn't said out loud in a long time.

The tape hissed softly between songs. She shifted beside me, then went still again.

The rest of camp passed without incident. We attended sessions, ate together and packed our bags. On Sunday afternoon, we walked out of the church centre and went our separate ways. Nothing had been said. Nothing had been fixed.

For the first time, I understood that silence wasn't just something you kept. It was something you lost people to.

***

12 - THE THING SHE DOESN'T ASK TWICE

TRISH was sitting on the low concrete ledge near the bus stop, her school bag resting beside her instead of on her shoulders, as if she had decided, at least for that moment, not to be in a hurry to be anywhere else. I hadn't expected to see her there. I had been moving quickly, mind already elsewhere, rehearsing reasons I didn't intend to give, answers to questions I hoped would not be asked.

She looked up when she heard my footsteps. She always recognised my pace before she saw me. That was something I never understood until much later—how familiarity isn't built on grand gestures, but on the small, repeated details we stop noticing because they feel permanent.

"Hey," she said, smiling, though there was a hesitation in it, a slight delay between recognition and warmth.

"Hey," I replied, stopping in front of her, already aware of how guarded my voice sounded, how careful.

For a moment, neither of us said anything. The silence wasn't awkward, not yet. It was the kind we had grown used to—the comfortable pause before conversation settled into its rhythm. Except this time, the rhythm didn't come.

"You've been hard to catch lately," she said eventually, not accusing, not even disappointed, just stating a fact the way you might comment on the weather or the time.

I shrugged, a reflex by then. "School's been busy."

She nodded, accepting the answer too easily. That should have unsettled me more than it did.

"I thought maybe," she continued, tapping her fingers lightly against the concrete, "we could all go cycling this weekend. East Coast. Mike said he might be free."

She didn't look at me when she said it. She stared straight ahead, as if offering the suggestion into the open air rather than placing it directly between us. It was a safe invitation—public, ordinary, familiar. The kind we had relied on for months to keep things uncomplicated.

"Yeah," I said, too quickly. Then, after a pause that felt necessary but added nothing, "I'll see."

I didn't say no. I didn't say yes. I said the one

thing that required no commitment and carried no consequence, at least not immediately.

She turned to look at me then, really look at me, as if something in my tone had finally confirmed what she had been sensing for some time.

"Are you okay?" she asked.

The question landed softly, but it wasn't casual. It was careful, deliberate. She wasn't asking about my day or my studies or whether I was tired. She was asking about the space that had opened between us—the one neither of us had named.

I could have told her then. Not everything. Not the market or the altar or the joss sticks. But something. Anything that acknowledged the distance without pretending it wasn't there.

Instead, I did what I had learned to do best.

"I'm just figuring some things out," I said.

It sounded reasonable. Mature, even. The kind of answer people accept because it doesn't demand further explanation.

She held my gaze for a moment longer than usual. Her expression didn't change, but something behind it did—a subtle recalibration, as if she were adjusting her expectations in real time.

"Okay," she said finally.

There was no disappointment in her voice. No frustration. That, too, should have alarmed me.

We stood there a while longer, talking about nothing in particular—a competition her club was preparing for, a song she had heard on the radio, how crowded the buses had been lately. Ordinary things. Safe things. The kind of conversation you have when both people are carefully avoiding what matters most.

When it was time to leave, she picked up her bag and slung it over her shoulder in one smooth motion, the decision already made.

“See you,” she said.

“Yeah,” I replied.

“See you.”

She took a few steps, then stopped and turned back.

“` Lan,” she said.

I looked up.

“If you ever want to talk—really talk—just let me know.”

It wasn’t a plea. It wasn’t even a request. It was an offering, made plainly and without conditions.

I nodded.

“Okay.”

She smiled, smaller than before, and left.

She didn’t look back.

It took me a long time to understand what had

happened at that moment. At the time, I told myself nothing had changed—that we would talk again, that things would settle, that whatever this unease was, it would pass on its own. I believed, foolishly, that closeness was something you could pause and resume at will, like a song stopped midway and restarted without losing its shape.

What I didn't understand was that she had asked the question she needed to ask—not out loud, but through patience, through presence, through the quiet consistency of someone willing to wait only as long as waiting still made sense.

She did not ask it twice.

There are moments in life that do not announce themselves as turning points. They do not come with raised voices or slammed doors or final words that echo long after they are spoken. They pass gently, almost kindly, leaving nothing more than the faint awareness that something essential has shifted.

By the time I realised what I had lost, she was already moving forward—not away from me, exactly, but toward a version of herself that did not depend on my readiness.

And I was left standing where I had always stood, mistaking silence for safety, and distance for control, unaware that the very thing I was trying to protect myself from had already begun to claim its price.

***

13 - LET SLEEPING DOGS LIE

MICHAEL was first to notice that Trish had appeared in his school more regularly after classes. He glanced at her while walking to the canteen. It surprised him, but then again, people were always coming and going. Then he recognised the other girls that she was together with and deduced, "Ahh, club meeting." So he positioned himself carefully in the walkway so that they would run into each other.

"Hey Trish," he called out casually as he passed her and startled her.

"Oh, Hi Mike!" she rang out a cheery greeting.

She was at his school to prepare for the upcoming division club competition and both schools were teaming up. As club captain, she would be in his school more often to plan and rehearse. They would have joint training at school grounds. This confirmed what he had worked out on his own earlier.

"Wow, that's really cool and exciting!" Michael quipped in his usual way.

"Maybe we'll get to hang out after school?"

"Okay, we'll see," Trish replied in a measured manner.

Michael noticed the drop in tone of her voice but he didn't show it. He knew it was negative based on her reply. He could understand that she didn't want him in her club orbit or even near it. Besides, she would be staying late and that was something that he didn't do.

The following week, it happened again. She showed up in school with her club members and was rehearsing again. This time, he didn't want to be nosy and disappeared into the hallways and avoided contact. He knew enough not to be seen or heard in that social space. And besides, he had other things to tend to.

In the late afternoon, as he was leaving school, he noticed that Trish was sitting closely with another guy alone. They seemed intense in their conversation, talking over a sheet of paper. But their body language told him another story.

"These two are getting pret-ty close," he muttered to himself.

Her face lit up whenever she spoke to him and when he replied, she smiled or made a small laugh. He was gesturing and brushed her arms and hands occasionally. It felt intimate and he was wondering to himself what was going on.

"Was this Trish's new boyfriend?" he wondered.

Sometimes, I would call Michael for no apparent reason in the evening. I would check on plans for the weekend or just talk about nothing in general. The conversations would usually last an hour or until my dad asked me to hang up.

"Hey, I saw Trish at school again today," he said as a matter of factly, assuming that I would already know about this.

Now Trish's school was very near Michael's and the students shared a common bus stop. They were bound to bump into each other at some point during the week.

"Oh, did you see her at the bus stop?" I asked without much thought.

"I thought you knew—she was in my school, preparing for the divisional competition. She comes every week," he said.

"Yeah, she told me about it," I replied.

But it was the first I heard of it. Trish didn't mention this at all.

"She's hanging around with the St. John's guys and the captain, doing some planning and stuff," Michael stated.

"Does she have a boyfriend or something?"

Michael asked.

"No, why?" I asked back.

"Well, it certainly looked like she was pretty close to the club captain," Michael said with a neutral stance.

He knew about me and Trish being just *brother* and *sister* and that there was nothing going on with the two of us. Or was there?

"Oh and another thing, " he suddenly tightened up.

It wasn't his place to say something to put anyone down and he certainly did not want to interfere with anyone's business. He didn't want to poke his nose where it didn't belong, but in this case, because it was me, perhaps for once, he would cross the line. It wasn't something he did lightly either.

"I actually heard from some people that this guy bragged about getting into some girl's pants soon," he said with an air of concern.

It wasn't Michael to spread rumours, but if he dropped a statement like that—it was something that weighed on him.

I was thinking the same thing that he was thinking—the girl was Trish.

***

14 - THE PRICE OF POWER

AT school, I began to recognise other gang members—boys from different classes, different homes. Some came from humble backgrounds: sons of vegetable vendors or fishermen. I knew one whose parents ran a fried carrot cake stall in the wet market. They were still students, doing the best they could, staying out of trouble.

As we passed one another in the school hallways, we traded brief glances and small nods, but never acknowledged each other openly with secret handshakes or coded words. Nothing was said, yet everything was understood. Everyone knew one another's affiliations, but no one spoke about them aloud. Loyalty bound us together quietly.

The police dealt with any triad or gang affiliation severely. This included detention without trial. Strangely, while we kept everything hidden, it was often the boys without any real societal affiliations who caused the most trouble. They formed their own street gangs and harassed others—sometimes for money, sometimes for possessions. They were bolder, more reckless, and openly aggressive. Intimidation was their currency.

Those with real power, however, stayed calm. There were consequences for public displays of bullying and recklessness. Internal discipline was swift—reprimands, penalties, and punishments that sometimes involved kneeling before seniors to seek forgiveness. Because of this hierarchy and sense of order, the boys from the societies were more restrained. Matters were discussed, not rushed. Action was deliberate. Power was a means to an end, not an excuse for wanton aggression or retaliation.

There was an incident when a boy from a street gang harassed a student from another class through a prolonged stare, provoking a challenge. He openly bragged about his gang ties. What he didn't know was that the victim had societal affiliations. The matter was brought to a senior in an older class, and it was decided that it had to be resolved. Respect had to be enforced.

A meeting was arranged after school, in a back alley opposite the school. The street gang showed up—about five of them, including the aggressor. The victim quietly mobilised members of his affiliation from within the school, myself included. We numbered twenty.

At the start of the confrontation, there was an uncomfortable silence between the aggressor and the victim.

"Why were you staring at me?" the aggressor asked.

"Why, can't I?" challenged the victim.

They locked eyes, chests raised, fists clenched, attempting to intimidate one another. As more of us gathered around, it became clear that we had outnumbered them. I can't remember who threw the first shove. Everything blurred quickly into chaos.

The fight was over almost as soon as it began. All five were knocked down. The larger group continued kicking them.

"Stop!" the lookout shouted.

We dispersed as quickly as we had gathered. I walked home fast—afraid of being identified, anxious to disappear, utterly alone in the aftermath. That day, the victim became the victor.

The five boys were never seen lingering outside the school gates again. They kept their heads down and went straight home once the bell rang. They knew better.

Power had been demonstrated—and enforced. If those five were ever seen near any of us again, it would mean trouble. That invisible boundary was enough to keep them away. It only worked as long as everyone remembered it.

After that incident, I was quietly but firmly identified as someone with associations, and harassment now came with consequences. The bullying stopped completely. But it came at a cost.

I now led a double life: a church-going altar boy in Sunday classes, and a member of a secret society by night. The contrast was jarring. I had gained power, but I was no longer carefree. Every action had to be measured, every word guarded. I felt awkward in my own skin, unsure how to behave.

***

15 - THE QUIET SHIFT

FOR a while, nothing happened.

After the night at Six Mile, after the smoke and incense and the bowing that didn't mean anything to me, I kept waiting for the world to tilt or crack open. I expected school to swallow me whole. I expected the boys who used to follow me, the ones who liked to brush past my shoulder too hard, the ones who laughed when my bag tore or my shoes were ruined, to sense something on me and come looking. I expected consequences.

No, none of them came. That was the strange part.

Instead, the days arrived like they always had—humid mornings, uniforms that never quite dried properly, the smell of canteen food clinging to our hands, teachers talking over the noise like it was normal. The bell rang, we filed into class, and the ceiling fans pushed warm air around in circles that never cooled anything. Everything looked the same.

But how people moved around me changed.

It wasn't obvious. There was no announcement, no badge. Nothing about me looked tougher. I was still skinny, still smaller than most, still carrying my books the same way, elbows tucked in like I was trying not to take up space. If you looked at me quickly you would have seen the same boy. But if you watched the people around me, you could see it in the small adjustments—shoulders angling away, eyes sliding off, conversations going quiet for a second and then returning when I passed.

At first I thought I was imagining it. I told myself it was just luck. Maybe the bullies had found a new target. Maybe someone else had bought clean shoes. But the pattern was too neat to ignore.

But then it happened again, and again.

The group of boys who used to trail me on the bus —the same ones who stomped on my new shoes —suddenly disappeared from my routine. One day, on the bus ride home, I noticed that they were already standing at the back when I climbed the steps. I saw them before they saw me. They were leaning into each other, laughing loudly and bashfully, that same kind of laughter that didn't need a joke. My stomach tightened the way it always did, automatically, like my body knew before my mind could react.

One of them glanced up.

His face shifted. It was subtle, like a flicker of something passing across his eyes—calculation, recognition, uncertainty. He nudged the boy beside him and said something I couldn't hear. The boy turned, looked at me, and his mouth went flat. They didn't stare. They didn't grin. They looked away.

The space near them opened as if by accident. Not a generous opening. Not an invitation. Just enough for me to pass.

I walked down the aisle slowly, forcing myself not to rush, forcing my steps to land evenly even though my hands were cold and my heartbeat was loud. I took a seat nearer the front. I didn't turn around again. But I could feel the difference like a draft—like the air behind me had changed direction.

At school, it was the same.

The corridor outside my classroom was always crowded, boys brushing past each other, pushing, shouting, playing rough the way they did when no teacher was close enough to hear. In the past, someone would have clipped my shoulder on purpose or slapped the back of my head as they ran by. It was never a big act. It was a hundred small ones, designed to remind you where you stood.

Now, people keep their hands to themselves.

Not everyone. Some boys still tried their luck

with others. But with me, there was a caution I had never earned. Sometimes a boy would look at me too long and then drop his eyes. Sometimes a laugh would cut off halfway, like someone pinched it shut.

There was some relief in it. I won't pretend there wasn't.

For the first time in years, I could go a day without bracing my shoulders. I could sit in class and actually listen instead of scanning the room. I could wait for the bell without feeling like I was waiting to be chosen. It was like someone had lowered the volume of the world, and I could finally hear myself think. But with that relief came something else. Fear, again. Just a different kind. Before, I was afraid of being hurt. Now, I was afraid of being seen.

Because whatever had shifted in the school corridors and on the bus rides didn't come from me. It came from something I had stepped into, something I didn't fully understand and couldn't fully control. It was power that didn't belong to my body. It belonged to a name I wasn't allowed to speak, to a set of faces that appeared only at night, to rules that were never written down but always enforced. And now that it had touched me, I had to carry it carefully.

I began to watch myself as I watched everyone else.

I measured the way I laughed. I watched my tone. I kept my head down without seeming ashamed. I avoided looking too nervous, but I also avoided looking too confident. Confidence invited questions. Questions were dangerous.

When teachers spoke to me, I replied politely, quickly, with as few words as possible. I didn't want to draw attention. When classmates asked what I did after school, I shrugged and said, "Nothing much." That became my favourite answer. It ended conversations before they could go anywhere.

At home, my parents were tired. They came back late with the smell of the shop still on them—fabric and sweat and the faint dust that clung to clothing after a long day. My mother's hands were rough from work. My father's face looked older than it had a year ago. They asked the usual questions—Did you eat? Any homework?—and I answered the way a dutiful son should. I became good at being unremarkable. My brothers were in their worlds. They barely looked up. It wasn't hard to disappear in my own house.

And yet, in the small spaces between days, there were moments when I almost reached for someone. Sometimes, after dinner, I stood by the phone and stared at it. The receiver sat there like a simple thing, innocent, not knowing what kind of trouble it could carry. I would think of Tricia's voice—

how she laughed through the line, how she said my name like it belonged somewhere safe. I would imagine calling her, asking how her club practices were going, letting the conversation drift back into music the way it used to.

But then the other part of my mind would rise, cold and firm. If she asked where I had been, what would I say? If she heard something, if rumours reached her, if someone spoke too much and she repeated it without meaning harm—what then?

The code wasn't complicated. It was just absolute. No names. No statements. No questions. Silence was loyalty.

I hung up the receiver without picking it up.

On Sundays, I still showed up at church sometimes. The stone walls and wooden pews were familiar enough that my body relaxed the moment I stepped inside. The air was cooler there. The smell of incense didn't scare me like it did at Six Mile. Here, it felt clean, controlled, holy even. I slipped into the back the way I always did, keeping my eyes forward.

I would see Michael sometimes, and the sight of him would loosen something in my chest. He was still the same—bigger than me, awkward in his own way, eyes bright when music came up, always ready to talk about the latest song on the charts. When he waved, I waved back. I tried to smile like nothing had changed.

But I couldn't hold his gaze for long.

Because Michael was honest in a way I wasn't anymore. With him, I didn't have to calculate every word. We talked and talked until the world fell away. Now I felt like there was a wall in my mouth, built from things I couldn't say. He would tell me about a new album, a new remix someone had gotten, and I would nod, but my mind would be elsewhere—counting time, measuring distance, keeping track of who was near us.

After service, he would sometimes ask, "Are you coming for Sunday Class?"

I would say, "Maybe."

And then I wouldn't.

It wasn't that I hated the church. It wasn't that I had stopped believing, not exactly. It was that I no longer knew where I fit. The church wanted you to be one thing. Society wants you to be another. School wanted you to survive. Home wanted you to behave. I didn't feel brave enough to choose a direction, so I floated between them, hoping nobody would pull too hard. The worst part was that, for a while, it worked.

A week went by, then another. The bullying stayed away. My school bag stayed intact. Nobody stepped on my shoes. Nobody grabbed me by the collar for fun. I started to carry myself differently—not proudly, but less flinching. I had space. I had breath.

For some reason or another, the guy from my class who had broken my pencil case now started to avoid me. Everyday, I would go about my business in school and I subtly noticed that he had stopped going after me. Once, during recess, he brushed his shoulder against mine. His eyes met mine for half a second. He didn't smile. He didn't nod openly. But his chin dipped, just slightly. A gesture so small it could have been nothing.

Except it wasn't nothing. My stomach tightened, as it always did when I encountered him. But this time he left and left me alone.

I kept walking, not faster, not slower. My face stayed blank. But inside, something had clicked into place. This was the new life now. Not being hurt did not mean being safe. It meant being claimed.

That night, lying in bed, I listened to the sounds of my neighbourhood settling into sleep—the neighbour's television muffled through the wall, someone's footsteps above, the distant motorbike revving and fading. I waited for music to rise in my head, the way it usually did, some chorus looping itself into comfort.

Nothing came.

Only the memory of Six Mile market at night, the glow of a Taoist altar, the heat of joss sticks in my fingers, and the knowledge that I had traded one fear for another. And in the silence, I understood something I hadn't admitted to myself before. I hadn't joined because I wanted to be powerful. I had joined because I was tired of being powerless. And that tiredness—more than any senior, more than any rule, more than any oath—was what frightened me most.

Quietly, I withdrew—from my family, from my friends, and especially from Trish. I kept everything closer to my chest than ever.

***

PART II

16 - FOUR MINUTES OF LIGHT

JUST before midnight on Christmas Eve in 1985, our entire Sunday class cohort was Confirmed. It was not only an affirmation of our faith in the Catholic Church; for many of us, it was also a rite of passage—from childhood into adolescence. Before this, there were few milestones in our small lives. We went to school, sat for exams, and repeated the cycle year after year. But this was different. We had spent two years in Sunday classes, church camps, and retreats preparing for this day, and it felt significant.

The Rite of Confirmation took place midway through the Christmas Eve Mass. I was both a Confirmand and part of the Mass service as an altar boy. We were all dressed in white—the girls in white dresses, the boys in white shirts and trousers. To mark the special occasion, the parish priests wore white vestments trimmed with gold, and the altar boys wrapped special gold sashes around their waists. The Archbishop was the celebrant. He carried a golden sceptre and wore a mitre —a tall, pointed ceremonial headdress. I had never seen one so close, and I was thrilled.

A grand procession of over eighty youths walked from the church entrance to the altar, led by the Archbishop and flanked by parish priests and altar boys. It was a spectacle for the entire local Catholic community. Because it was Christmas, the church was packed with families and parishioners. During the Rite, each Confirmand stepped forward to be anointed with holy oil by the Archbishop.

I sneaked out when the first person was being Confirmed, and scanned the congregation quickly for Victor and the others. They should have been there. Even though they had joined the cohort late, I still expected them to be Confirmed along with the rest of us. But I didn't see him all night. Perhaps I had simply missed him. Taking off my cassock quickly, I joined the others and waited for my turn.

"Alan, be sealed with the gift of the Holy Spirit," the Archbishop said as he anointed my forehead with holy oil and smiled gently.

"Amen," I replied.

"Peace be with you," he followed.

"And with your spirit," I responded.

And just like that, I was Confirmed. We had spent weeks rehearsing this simple exchange, to the laughter and distress of the Sunday class catechists. They made sure that none of us would mess this up on the day.

When the final Confirmand was anointed, the church erupted in applause. I threw my arms up and cheered with the rest of my cohort.

Michael found me after.

"Fun fact—the Archbishop shares the same surname as you," he pointed out.

I couldn't help but laugh. It was so Michael.

After Mass, the church spared no expense and hosted a Christmas and Confirmation party for the newly Confirmed, catechists, and parents. The church centre's main hall had been transformed into a full discotheque—streamers hung from the windows, rotating spotlights swept the room, mirror balls reflected light in every direction, and a smoke machine filled the air. Over two hundred and fifty people crammed into the hall to celebrate. A local radio DJ, who was also a parishioner, spun records that night, lending the event an added sense of occasion.

Hits from the 80s filled the dance floor as we gathered in small circles, dancing to *New Order* and *Bryan Adams' Summer of '69*. Then, midway through the night, a familiar five-note jingle rang out, followed by a beat everyone recognised instantly. *Everybody Wants To Rule The World.* The hall erupted in screams as we danced to its rhythm. For those four minutes, it felt like nothing could touch us—as though the world had paused to watch.

Trish, Michael, and our friends stayed together the whole night, dancing in the same circle as if nothing else mattered. There was still no sign of Victor, but it didn't seem important then. We took turns stepping into the centre of the circle, being silly—kicks, exaggerated gestures, anything to make each other laugh. Breakdancing was all the rage, and we attempted moves that earned groans and laughter in equal measure. Michael and I sang every song. As music nerds, we had memorised lyrics from everyone, from *Pet Shop Boys* to *A Flock of Seagulls*.

Midway through the night, we were allowed one slow dance—on the condition that our bodies did not touch. When *Madonna's Crazy for You* played, I had my first slow dance with Trish. I didn't need to ask—she moved toward me instinctively. We kept our distance, but her hands rested around my sweat-soaked neck while mine hovered lightly at her waist as we swayed.

Even though we had been drifting apart lately, we still cherished each other's company. We shared that moment—renewal of faith, friendship, and something unspoken. Few words were exchanged. Maybe none were needed.

“Lan, you’ve changed,” she said quietly. After a long pause, she asked, “Do you think after ten years, we’ll remember this night and still be friends?”

I didn’t answer. I could only manage a faint smile, fighting back tears. That night, I forgot the duality of my life and allowed myself to enjoy it fully. It was a night I would always remember. We would never return to that moment or experience it the same way again.

That night, I crossed from being a shy fourteen-year-old into someone a little more sure of himself—someone who had found his footing among friends, yet still unsure of where life would lead with the decisions that I made.

Later, I learned that Victor and the others had decided not to be Confirmed at all. They skipped it entirely.

Well—maybe next year.

***

17 - THE LONG WAY OUT

AFTER Confirmation, we were encouraged to return to Sunday classes for another two years, until we turned sixteen. They called it the Youth Group. Many didn't return, choosing instead to do something else. Less than half of the cohort came back, and we were left with a much smaller group. This was expected. Those who had formed friendships stayed; those who hadn't were never seen again.

For many Catholics like me, going to church was more of a social norm than religious conviction. We were baptised as infants, sent to Sunday classes from Primary One, and attended Mass with our families because it was expected. It was something families did together, not necessarily something deeply believed in. Some joined church organisations—ministries, as they were called—to explore further. Others simply didn't. After eight to ten years of Sunday school, many felt it was enough. Friendship, more than faith, was what kept people around. Deeper beliefs, if they came at all, tended to develop later in life.

After Confirmation, the church encouraged us to join its various ministries in the hope that we would put down deeper roots. During Youth Group, there were mini roadshows where different ministries recruited new members. The more popular ones were the Lectors, who read Scripture during Mass, and the Sunday Choir, which drew the largest numbers each year.

Michael joined the Lectors. He was stoic, intellectual and loved to read. The ministry appealed to his thoughtful, nerdy nature. It was a place where order mattered, words had boundaries, and no one asked him to intervene. They practised public speaking, diction, and reading confidently before the congregation. It was focused on individual development and suited him well.

Trish, along with many others, joined the Sunday Choir. It was more dynamic and group-oriented. There was a kind of herd instinct—if one joined, the rest followed. Music was central to our lives in the 80s, and choir felt like a natural extension of that. They sang contemporary praise and worship songs, led the congregation, rehearsed with live bands, and organised outings. It was lively, social, and it suited Trish.

I didn't want to join either. After the emotional high of Confirmation, I felt myself slipping into a slow, steady decline. Whatever connection I had to church felt complete, even spent. It wasn't doubt that pulled me away. It was fatigue—the kind that comes from holding too many versions of yourself at once. I didn't want to commit to something that no longer excited me. My parents hardly went to church on Sundays, and I no longer had a group anchoring me there.

I drifted away —always searching for belonging but never settling. I moved from group to group, unable to commit, unwilling to move as part of a herd. There was school, the society, Youth Group, altar boys, and now ministries. Everything felt crowded and emotionally complicated. I didn't want to belong to anything anymore.

Instead, I spent more time with Victor and his friends, especially after school. Even though they hadn't been Confirmed, I didn't feel divided from them. To them, Confirmation wasn't essential. When I asked Victor how he felt about skipping it, he shrugged it off. I doubted he ever intended to return. He had dropped out of Sunday classes entirely.

Victor was on a different path. He revelled in the power his affiliation gave him—the secrecy, the security, the loyalty that money alone could not buy. He wanted more, and he never questioned where he belonged. That certainty made him seem ahead of everyone else. It didn't occur to me then that certainty could also be a dead end. But I was drawn to his confidence because I lacked my own. I was still seeking identity, status, power.

I called Trish less often, went to Youth Group less frequently, and did the bare minimum as an altar boy, before leaving altogether. She left messages on the answering machine, wondering what I had been up to. I didn't return her calls.

Perhaps I was confused about what we were becoming. That night after Confirmation had been tender, but it left me emotionally exhausted. I wanted something deeper than *brother* and *sister.* I wanted exclusivity. But I didn't have the courage to say it. Social norms loomed heavily over young relationships, and I was afraid to cross that line. Avoidance became my solution. In my own way, I gave up on her.

I also gave up being Catholic—not abruptly, but gradually. I withdrew from church life the way many others had after Confirmation. The emotional tie that once bound me there had loosened, and I drifted away. Trish and Michael were the only two people I truly cared about, and both were moving in directions I didn't want to follow. I was torn between them, unable to choose. So I chose neither.

Months later, Trish left another message. This time, I returned her call the next day. From the start, something felt different. After months apart, I felt like an outsider. Her voice was restrained, cautious—no longer the bright, easy tone I remembered. It felt like she knew something but wouldn't say it.

"So what have you been doing?" she asked.

"Nothing much," I replied. It has become my default answer.

"Have you been hanging out with Victor and those guys?"

I didn't want to lie. But I didn't want to tell the truth either. Telling her would mean breaking the code—and pushing her further away.

"Yeah, sometimes," I said.

"I heard a rumour that those guys have gang affiliations," she said carefully, then paused.

I almost told her everything. I almost trusted her with the truth. I almost told her I wanted more from us. But I couldn't. Silence, in that moment, felt safer. Perhaps to her, silence was confirmation enough.

She changed the subject quickly, asking what I was doing in May. It was her birthday, and she invited me to her party. Then, unexpectedly, she asked about a guy she had been spending time with—someone from Michael's school. They were preparing together for a club competition in June. She asked what I thought of him, as if asking permission.

She was talking about Trent.

I hadn't thought much about him, except for what Michael had confirmed—that Trish had been seen with him after school. He was the club captain. Tall, confident, surrounded by admirers. Popular. But something ate me up inside about what Michael had told me about him—the way he talked about girls and the rumour about what he was planning to do.

There was a pause—just long enough for me to choose my words, and just short enough to fail.

"I think he's an asshole. I think you should stay away from him."

***

18 - THE CENTRE OF GRAVITY

THERE were two things that were really important to Trish in her life—school and St. John's—her club. Church was something that she grew up with and it was always in the background of her life. Sometimes she felt like she needed to be present in church to appease her parents. She noticed lately, distantly, that she no longer prayed about her decisions—she planned them. But her life now evolved around her friends in school and her involvement with her club.

She gave her all to the club, driving its activities as the club captain, working with the teacher-in-charge closely to schedule the weekly activities for its members, planning local and district competitions and attending to her constituent's needs. Since joining the club, she had risen quickly through the ranks and was the Captain. She was very proud of what she achieved. The club defined her identity—not the church. Without it, she lacked purpose, structure and discipline.

District competitions were held once a year and all schools had a chance to participate. There was an individual school event, and an area event—which clubs were allowed to partner with another school in the same area to compete. Trish was given the opportunity to lead this year's District competition and she was thrilled.

Her teacher-in-charge had strong connections with Michael's school club, and after some discussions, they jointly agreed to let both schools work together to compete jointly in the area event. That meant they would have to travel to the other school for practices. They had lacked the space and facilities in their own school and the other school was bigger and had a better setup. So once a week, Trish and her team would go to Michael's school to meet with their school club counterparts and rehearse.

Trish first met Trent then. Both had dynamic personalities and were both captains of their own teams. Outside of church, this was the first time that she had met anyone else of the opposite sex, and in a school environment. Trent was taller than her, had a wide smile and broad shoulders.

She immediately took to him for his looks and charismatic behaviour. He was attentive to her, made quick jokes about everything and had a nice wide smile. He was easy to get along with and all her ideas were easily discussed and accepted by him.

Their rehearsals were tough—drills were complicated and all their movements were self choreographed, which made it especially difficult for her and Trent. At the end of every session, they were exhausted but they were able to improve themselves with each practice and were getting better. The guys had followed Trent's leadership without reservation, which made it easier for her when her ideas were introduced to the routine.

Over time, the two bonded over the many weeks of planning and practice. Despite putting in long hours, they were both happy and satisfied with the results so far and felt that they were making good progress.

Sometimes, she would get on the phone in the evening and call Trent, excited about a new idea that she would have for the drill and they would work into the night to refine it before presenting it back to the team at the next practice. She would look forward to talking to Trent by phone, night after night.

She couldn't help but compare school club and church, friends from both parts of her life, and of course, me and Trent. We have been close, but lately, she was speaking less and less to me and more and more with Trent. I was absent and unavailable, didn't return her calls sometimes, but

Trent was always there. They had the competition and there was a sense of shared mission and purpose. Occasionally, she would hesitate with the receiver in her hand, wondering if she should call me —and then tell herself she'd do it later.

I existed in a world—church—that she had taken for granted. It has and will always be part of her life, whether she likes it or not. But school and club are at the forefront of her purpose right now, and she was driven because of that. She didn't think of it as choosing one person over another. It just felt like her days were filling up, and I was no longer where her energy went first. I was her *brother* and lent emotional support when needed. She didn't need me now—Trent was the "now". But she didn't complain outwardly that I was gradually becoming unavailable to her. She guessed that it was just this phase of her life right now and she needed to focus. But the growing distance between her and me was bottled inside.

Every week, as they got together, she would find herself closer to Trent. He's there and wants them to succeed.

After a late training session one day, while she was going through the last few adjustments to be made with Trent, their eyes met. She could smell his sweat and breath and didn't mind it. He was gesturing about how the routine would move and looking at him, she was distracted.

“Am I ready to be in a relationship? Who is right for me?” she asked herself.

That thought made her vulnerable and she touched her face and neck unconsciously, with that thought lingering.

Trent watched the way she touched her neck, the way her voice softened when she spoke. He smiled to himself—confident, unhurried—as if this was simply how things always went.

***

19 - THE MEASURE OF A LIFE

ONE Saturday, in the afternoon, sometime in the middle of March of 1986, I recalled walking home and noticed that everyone at the nearby coffee shop was crowding over the radio. Something was buzzing and it piqued my interest. Curious, I poked my head in and listened.

"Hotel New World, located at the corner of Serangoon Road and Owen Road, has collapsed completely. No news about survivors yet," I heard.

I was stunned.

I went downtown sometimes to watch movies with Trish, Michael and our church friends and were familiar with the area. It was one of our special activities together and we organised group dates to watch Hollywood blockbusters. The location of the building was near the theatre. The crowd at the coffee shop shook their heads in disbelief. No one spoke much. Some had tears in their eyes. The news was still developing, and everyone leaned closer to the radio, as if proximity might change what they were hearing.

I ran home and called my parents at the shop. My dad was on the phone and he responded in awe, "Really?"

I called Michael and Trish after that and we spent hours talking about it that day. Trish, who was passionate about first-aid as captain of her school's St. John's, was naturally concerned. We wondered if they had found any survivors—it was rumoured that as many as 300 people could have been trapped in the building.

The next day on Sunday, it was all over the headlines of the local newspapers. Up till that point, it was the largest disaster that affected Singapore. An entire building had collapsed in a moment without notice and was reduced to rubble.

I was deeply affected by the tragedy and something drew me to Sunday Mass that day. During church service, the entire congregation prayed for the safety of the survivors of the tragedy and asked everyone to help in one way or another, especially in blood donations. I felt that I had to do something but I didn't know what.

Trish, Michael and I met after service that day and decided that the three of us would take a bus together to the site. We wanted to experience what was happening first-hand. Trish wanted to offer any help, if possible. The more we talked about it, the deeper were our feelings.

Along the way, we bought the special noon edition of the local paper, which had the latest news. On the long bus ride, we shared its pages with each other and talked about the articles endlessly. It was like old times - going back and forth about the latest facts.

We got off the bus from a distance and slowly made our way to the site of the collapse. As we moved closer and closer, we noticed the large pile of concrete and rubble on the corner of the junction, where the building once was. It was chaos.

Ambulances were parked by the side, police were directing traffic as vehicles were diverted away from the site and the entire fire service was actively working to recover any remaining survivors that were buried. There were so many onlookers and bystanders—some were curious about what was going on, some were shouting out names of the missing.

I saw people seated by the side of the road, motionless while some others were attended by ambulance staff. There were mammoth cranes and hovering helicopters trying to lift major parts of the collapsed structure carefully so that rescuers could safely access those trapped. It was such a sight that it took us a while to comprehend it. Trish and Michael just stood there and were stunned by all of it.

"`Lan—what..." she said in a trembling voice.

"I know," I replied as I watched, unable to fathom the horror in front of me.

"What happened?" muttered Michael.

We held hands and watched silently in horror.

As news poured out from site—about 60 were still trapped—26 hotel staff and 16 bank staff were unaccounted for. I reflected on the fragility of life that day and the pointless challenges and fights we would have in our neighborhood. None of that mattered at that point.

Rescuers fought tirelessly to save lives late into the night at the risk of their own well being. We had spent weeks measuring ourselves against one another—staring too long, saying the wrong thing, defending nothing that mattered—while strangers lay alone under concrete, waiting to be found. Forty-two families were missing a father, mother, sister, brother.

I wondered then whether we valued our lives differently. Or whether we had simply forgotten what they were worth.

The three of us left the scene after a long while. Our heads bowed low, stirred by images of the site that would haunt us for many years to come. We were helpless—as teenagers, there was nothing much we could do but pray for the lives of those that were still trapped and hope for their safe return.

The next day, I went to school and continued my interest in the accident. But it affected not everyone. School continued as it did, lessons went on and students were mostly oblivious to the entire tragedy. I noticed the classmate that destroyed my pencil case was missing from class that day. Frankly, I thought nothing about him except to instinctively avoid him. I thought that he was malingering again.

There was news of a 19 year old girl being the first to be recovered under the collapsed hotel. In school, those who were following the news celebrated with pumped fists. Her rescuer had pulled her slowly, inch by inch to safety. She was not much older than us and worked as a receptionist. It was only 30 years later that she finally met her hero, a firefighter, and they shared a solemn, quiet embrace.

It had taken them six days of working around the clock to save anyone trapped under the debris, and many more months to clear what was left behind.

I later learned his mother was one of the tragedy's victims. She was a bank clerk that had worked in the bank that was in Hotel New World. She, along with 33 others, died that day. As for my classmate, he was never the same after the building collapse. He hung his head low, mostly kept to himself and went home alone after school. By the end of the year, he left the neighborhood and moved to another school.

The news of what happened to him made me sad.

***

20 - WHAT HE THINKS HE'S PROTECTING

TRENT finds himself thinking about Trish more and more. After spending so much time with her, he's even starting to like her. He's had other relationships before with other girls. He didn't try so hard to make them fall in love with him. He just had to turn on his charm and everything would fall on his lap. It was that easy. And after a few months, when he got bored with them, he would ghost them and move on to the next one. Sometimes he would even roll with a few girls at the same time. This was normal for him over time.

"It's not you, it's me," was the line that he would use.

As cliche as it sounds, it worked, every single time.

But this one was different. He had to work extra hard. He kept it cordial at first. Friendly. Then he began creating moments alone with her. After all the rehearsals, practices and everything in between, she was not falling for him—yet.

She's giving out all the right signals, he thought. He felt the goosebumps on her hands, she's sweating on the neck, and every time he makes eye contact with her, she plays with her hair or touches her cheeks. But when he tries to move closer, she turns her head, looks down and pulls back. It was confusing him. Infuriating him.

He wonders what's holding her back. How can she make up her mind and cross over to him? His pursuit of her now turns to an obsession. When something cannot be obtained, the victory of obtaining it becomes sweeter. He didn't think of it as wanting her. He thought of it as finishing what had already started.

He was exhausting his bag of tricks now. His smile and charm could only go so far. His fake supportiveness and back-and-forth laughter has worn him down. He began to feel impatient. He needed something more drastic, something with a little more oomph. He wondered who else in her life could be keeping her from falling in love with him. He should scare or fend off his rivals before they get close to her. After all, he was a winner and everyone else was a loser.

Late one evening, after another joint rehearsal with Trish and the team, the both of them ended up staying back and finishing up while everyone had left. It was growing late but there wasn't any urgency to leave. Trent and Trish lingered, as if there were words to be said that hadn't been said.

Trish was a little flustered today. She didn't seem herself and something was weighing on her mind throughout practice. She kept missing positions and timings, and apologised constantly. This was unlike her usual sharp, disciplined self.

"Hey, what's going on?" Trent was a little frustrated.

"What do you mean?" Trish pushed back a little.

"You're mistimed today and kept missing sequences."

After a long pause—"Sorry, I'm just a little distracted today," she confessed, getting a little flustered and bothered.

She began recounting a conversation she had with her *brother* from church. She explained their relationship to him and that they weren't related, but due to their closeness, they acknowledged each other as siblings. It was complicated.

"He is so frustrating. He never returns my calls when I ask him. When I need emotional support, he's not there. And when I talk about the district competition preparations, he seems like he's not really interested to listen. I don't know what's up with him. He said something about you last night and I bet he doesn't even know you," she ranted on and on.

"I don't know why he said that. He didn't even explain himself," she continued.

"Wait, what did he say?" Trent's ego was hurt now, indirectly. Someone called him something.

"He said you were an asshole," Trish blurted. Ouch, that hurt Trent's pride.

But here, in the emotional outburst, Trent thought something was happening. Has she turned on this guy and has now crossed over to him? Was this an opportunity for him to step in? As she ranted more and more about him, he noticed that her tone was becoming more and more distressed, fragile and vulnerable. He put his arms on her shoulder and this time, she did not flinch or turn away. She seemed comforted. She didn't pull away when he stood closer. Much closer.

Immediately after Trish said that, she regretted it. Her loyalties were tested and she felt she failed miserably. She didn't try to justify them, she was confused about what she was feeling at the moment. She questioned why she should be so upset with what her *brother* had said, how easily she dismissed him and why it affected her so much. But in the moment with Trent, she didn't want to face it. She faded away. Maybe she just wanted someone to listen to her.

Trent felt like he had won a prize that evening.

Everything was finally coming to plan. He started to trash talk about this *brother* of hers and she responded with small, uncertain smiles, the kind that perhaps came more from exhaustion than agreement. But he continued anyway, choosing to believe that he was winning her over. He saw that she needed affirmation and she received it willingly from him.

"Are we an item now?" thought Trent.

"So this was it, then," he concluded on his own.

In his mind, the way that she was offended when her *brother* spoke about Trent negatively. That suggests there is something there for sure. How could he have missed that? Was it premature? He told himself he was an expert at reading girls. In his experience, some girls didn't need to be asked if she agreed to be his girlfriend. Things were simply understood. It was implied consent and they would just start their relationship there.

Now it all made sense to him. This would mean that some guy called her boyfriend names and she was defending him. In turn, he needed to defend her honour as a girlfriend. This was the street code. He needed to do something to show his loyalty. If he can't protect his girlfriend then who else can? In his mind, this wasn't jealousy. It was his responsibility. She didn't ask him to do anything. But in his mind, he's expected to and already decided on the next course of action. He now ranked above her *brother*.

"Is he going to be at your birthday party next week?" Trent asked.

"Yeah," she said.

***

21 - DON'T DO ANYTHING STUPID

MICHAEL caught up with me just outside his school gates, his bag slung over one shoulder, walking with that familiar shuffle that made it hard to keep pace with him.

"Hey," he said, slightly out of breath.

"I'm heading off tomorrow."

"Tomorrow?" I asked.

"Where to?"

"Out of town. Family thing," he shrugged.

"A few days. Just for the weekend. I won't be around."

He said it lightly, the way he said most things, as if distance was temporary and life always resumed exactly where he left it.

"And I can't make it to Trish's birthday, so…"

He dug into his bag and pulled something out—small, wrapped in thin paper, carefully folded.

"Can you help me give this to Trish?" he said.

I took it from him, surprised by the weight of it in my hand.

"Yeah," I said.

"I'll tell her it's yours."

"Or maybe I should say it's mine," I teased him.

"Don't do that!"

"Thanks," he smiled.

"Tell her I said happy birthday. Don't let her think I forgot."

"Yeah, sure, I will."

We stood there for a moment, side by side, the late afternoon sun slanting across the pavement, buses pulling in and out of the stop nearby. A comfortable silence filled us, but it didn't linger long.

"She was in school again yesterday," Michael added casually, after a while.

"Club stuff. Trent is always around her now."

I looked at him and he raised a brow intentionally.

I nodded, though my stomach tightened into a knot.

"Yeah, you told me about it," I said, trying not to

sound too worried.

“It’s probably nothing,” he continued, already waving the thought away.

“People get busy. It’ll all settle down.”

That was Michael—assuming the world would arrange itself sensibly if left alone. He adjusted his bag strap and glanced back toward the road.

“Anyway,” he said.

“We’ll catch up when I’m back. Don’t do anything *stupid* while I’m gone.”

I laughed, maybe a little too quickly.

“Have a good trip,” I said, this time, wishing he would stay.

“You too,” he replied, and grinned, already half-turned away.

He walked off toward the bus stop, unhurried, humming something under his breath. His bus was here. I watched until he disappeared into the crowded bus, then looked down at the small package in my hand.

Michael was leaving town. I was staying behind. Where was my wingman when I needed him?

***

22 - THE STAIRWELL

I became increasingly anxious about Trish's birthday party. I didn't know what to wear. I hadn't bought her a present. And more importantly, I didn't know what time to show up. Too early, and I would sit awkwardly waiting for guests to arrive. Too late, and I would miss my chance to speak to her.

The party was set to start at 7 P.M. I thought maybe arriving an hour later would be appropriate.

"7.30. P.M." I finally decided.

Everyone from church would be there—her school club friends, and likely her counterpart school club friends she had been preparing for competition with. To add to my anxiety, Michael had been invited but his family was away that weekend.

I spent weeks preparing. I went to a local thrift

shop and combed through the aisles, searching for something to wear. While I was engrossed in the shelves, I felt a slap on my shoulder and looked up. It was Victor. He caught me completely off guard. He wasn't the type who shopped in places like this. He was dumpster diving, looking for high-end barely used speakers to add to his collection.

"So I heard Trish's having a birthday party," he said.

"Are you going?"

"I haven't decided," I said, trying to move on to something else.

There was tension between us. I knew he knew I was invited. I also knew he wasn't. They weren't friends, didn't speak to each other—why would he be invited? And I wasn't about to ask him or the guys to come along. I didn't want both universes to collide. And even if I did, I doubt they would come. Victor wouldn't go to parties like this. It was so uncool.

"Trent's going to be there," Victor said.

Oh. The school club captain.

"Yeah, I heard," I replied almost immediately, confirming what I already feared. The party suddenly felt heavier.

I left the thrift shop without buying anything. I just wanted out of this uncomfortable situation. The more I thought about the party, the less I wanted to go.

There was an unspoken truth about relationships then. If someone was interested in someone else, potential suitors would quietly step aside. It was considered honourable. But Trish and I were only *brother* and *sister.* That didn't signal exclusivity. She was fair game. So why did this feel so unbearable?

Before the party, I borrowed a shirt from Michael's brother. He was smaller than Michael but about my size. It was grey with thin blue vertical stripes. I thought it looked cool—something I might have seen on *Top of the Pops*. I paired it with khaki cargo pants, the kind with pockets hanging off the sides.

For her gift, I did something different. I spent a week recording a mixtape for her—songs we loved, songs we'd shared over long phone calls, holding the receiver up to the stereo so the other could hear. I remembered every song she liked. Borrowing the vinyls took time. Some came from Victor's collection, others from my brothers and their friends. I placed the cassette into a small gift box and slipped it into my pocket. I didn't plan to give it to her when I arrived. Maybe later. Maybe just before I left.

Her apartment entrance was draped with vertical rainbow-coloured streamers—the kind you had to part with your hands to walk through. Living room furniture had been pushed into the bedrooms to make space. Plastic chairs lined the walls, girls on one side, boys on the other. A mirror ball hung from the ceiling where the fan was, balloons everywhere. Her parents fussed over food in the kitchen and Trish was with them.

A simple cassette player sat in the corner, playing favourite songs as her friends took turns swapping tapes. It was simple, but perfect. I thought maybe this would be the moment I could give my gift in person and Michael's. She could use it right away.

Before I could even find her, Trent and his friends confronted me.

"So you're Alan," he said.

"We need to talk."

Along with four others, I was ushered outside into the apartment stairwell. It was dark and dim, with a weak fluorescent light in the ceiling. We came to a small landing and immediately, I was surrounded by them. There was tension in the air and I could hear a pin drop. The silence was deafening.

Some of the party followed, wondering what was going to transpire. They crowded around the stairs leading to the landing, squeezing against themselves to have a better look.

From inside, the chorus of *Everybody Wants To Rule The World* rang faintly, echoing with a strange reverb.

"You called me an asshole," he said, breaking the silence.

He was taller, aggressive. I couldn't look him in the eye.

I froze, hands shoved into my pockets, searching for something to hold. My fingers brushed against the gift box. My mind raced back to my last conversation with Trish.

"What did she tell him?" I thought.

The question hurt, as I realised how far apart we had drifted.

"Yeah. So what?" I said, trying to sound calm.

My hands trembled. Even though I had affiliations, I chose not to reveal them. Exposing myself felt worse. I let it happen.

"Say that you'll never, never, never, never need it. One headline, why believe it?" the song rang in the distance.

It happened so quickly I didn't have any time to react. Each of them took turns kicking my legs while everyone watched in horror. I tried to block myself by squatting, but the blows kept coming.

But I didn't feel pain—just humiliation.

"Stop!" a familiar voice shouted.

Out of the corner of my eye, I saw Trish. She was petrified. It was the first time I saw fear and hurt in her eyes. Our eyes met, just like during the Christmas slow dance—but this time, something was irrevocably different.

I quickly went down the stairs, with a small limp —but there wasn't a sharp pain anywhere. But emotionally, I was shattered. My mind raced and I just wanted out of there. As I reached into my pockets, I felt it—the gift box was crushed. I took it out and shook it—the sounds of the broken pieces rattled. The mixtape was destroyed. I never got the chance to give it to her.

I told myself this was all my fault.

But staying quiet had kept things from getting worse.

***

23 - THE COST OF BEING DEFENDED

THERE was so much confusion. One minute everyone was in the living room, the next minute, most of them had emptied into the stairwell. Trish was in the kitchen with her parents, helping with the food and didn't notice anything until she suddenly heard a low shuffling of feet. She surfaced from the kitchen into the living room and heard two loud voices that were familiar to her—her *brother's* and Trent.

Immediately she sensed something was up and bolted out of the apartment. She saw where everyone had gathered—to the stairwell. She made a small opening in the crowd and peered, not knowing what was going on. A small circle had formed in the middle. To her horror, her *brother* was in the centre of it, surrounded by Trent and his friends, and was being kicked.

Instinctively, with tears in her eyes, as loud as she could, she shouted 'Stop!'. And they did. Her *brother* fled the scene, quickly walking down the stairs.

“`Lan, wait!” she cried out to him but he didn’t hear anything. He was already out of sight. She forced herself through bystanders and ran after him. Within minutes, he had disappeared and she was left standing alone.

Humiliated, confused and deflated—she asked herself, “What just happened?”

Wiping her tears from her face, she made her way back to her apartment, but the mood of the party had changed. Everyone was looking at Trent and his friends. No one really knew who he or his friends were except her club friends. Trent was clearly rattled, felt ostracised and forced a smile as he reunited with Trish.

“He got what he deserved,” he said smugly.

“What have you done?” she demanded under her breath with reddened eyes. “I never wanted any of this.”

Trent felt out of place as more and more staring eyes were upon him. He was more confused at this point. He never had to explain himself, at least not to his *girlfriend*.

“Alright then,” he declared.

He put up a false bravado and left without a word. His friends followed.

Trish just wanted to hide in her room. Her party

had just imploded before it began. She didn't know where to begin to explain her feelings of defeat and embarrassment. She knew she had something to do with what she told Trent.

Trish's parents were deeply disappointed but didn't react to anything. There was going to be a time and a place to sort this matter out. And now wasn't the time nor the place. What was important was to resume the party as soon as possible, which they did. They pretended as if nothing had happened and continued hosting.

Soon everyone was back to normal—except Trish. She was angry that the fight had ruined her party, and said nothing more. The party continued, but she didn't. Food was served, cake was cut, music was played—but deep inside, she stood still. Her special day was frozen at that stairwell.

After the party, her thoughts lingered about her *brother*. She felt very sorry about what happened to him. In her moment of vulnerability, she allowed Trent to come between them. If she had seen him when he came, she told herself, she might have stopped it. She started blaming herself for what happened to him.

"It was my fault," she kept saying.

That night, she cried herself to bed, wondering how she would make everything right. She knew, somewhere beneath the guilt, that she hadn't asked for any of it.

At the next practice meet, their eyes didn't meet. Trish kept her interactions with Trent to the minimum. She didn't hide her feelings of being upset. It was another bad rehearsal, and this time, Trish had no mood to be part of it. Trent tried many times to initiate conversation, but she just ignored him, showing her displeasure on her face. After practice, he pulled her aside when everyone had left.

"Why are you avoiding me?" he demanded.

"If you have to ask me that, then you really don't know what's going on," she shot back.

"I was defending you as my girlfriend, that's what's going on," Trent said, waiting for some sense of affirmation from Trish.

But it never came, instead what happened next was beyond his understanding.

"Girlfriend? I'm not your girlfriend!"

Trent was really confused now. There were too many assumptions and conclusions he had made at this point. He thought his actions would have made her feel that she was protected. But it didn't. He tried to justify it by claiming he did it for her. But it backfired horribly, and now he wasn't sure what his next move was.

"You had no right to hit him. Just because I'm frustrated with him doesn't mean that you had to attack him," she said firmly with steeled eyes.

"What is wrong with you?" she continued.

In desperation, he reached for her, trying to pull her close. He wanted the intimacy like it was the last time they were alone. He thought he had permission. But she pushed him away. It was the first time any girl rejected him in such a way. He reacted. For a moment, she saw it—not in his words, but in his body. His jaw tightened, his hands curled, and the space between them felt suddenly unsafe. Frustration turned to anger and he glared at her. At that moment, she realised, with a sudden clarity, that the anger she was seeing wasn't new—it was just the first time it had been directed at her.

Without another word, Trent stormed off.

Trish didn't know how any of this had started, only that it now belonged to her. Trapped between a rock and a hard place—all she wanted was someone to listen to her. It was not the result she imagined. Her troubles had only begun. Her parents were going to complain about the fight to the boy's schools. She had to do something before it all went terribly wrong, especially for her *brother*.

***

24 - THE QUIET AFTER

AFTER Trish's party, every time I closed my eyes, the stairwell returned—its concrete walls, the echo of voices, the dull thud of shoes against my legs. The humiliation lingered longer than the pain. Pain fades. Humiliation settles.

I lay on my bed staring at the ceiling fan as it turned slowly, counting rotations the way I counted steps when I was nervous. One. Two. Three. My legs throbbed faintly, but it wasn't enough to explain the tightness in my chest. That came from somewhere else.

The moment replayed over and over again, wondering where exactly I had lost control. Was it when I spoke too freely to Trish? When I let myself believe that what we shared was protected? Or when I chose silence instead of power?

I could have stopped it. That was the part that gnawed at me. I knew who I was affiliated with. I knew what a single word, a single look, a single name could have done. The fight would never have happened. Or it would have ended differently. Quietly. Cleanly. With consequences that didn't involve five pairs of shoes and a broken cassette tape. I mistook restraint for control.

But I hadn't done that. Instead, I stood there with my hands in my pockets, holding on to something fragile while the rest of me was being reduced to nothing.

The mixtape.

That hurt more than I expected. It wasn't just music. It was time. It was our memories between us. Every song is carefully chosen, recorded late at night, volume adjusted by instinct. It was proof that I cared in a way I had never said out loud. Proof I wasn't brave enough to give. Now it was crushed, warped beyond repair, just like the night itself.

I wondered if Trish had meant to betray me. I didn't think she had. Not really. But intention didn't matter much once words left your mouth. They changed shape in other people's hands. I understand that now.

Still, the image of her standing there—frozen, pale, watching—refused to leave me. The look in her eyes wasn't judgment. It was fear. And something else. Regret, maybe. Or helplessness. I wondered if she cried after I left. That thought stayed with me longer than I wanted.

On Saturday morning, the house moved as it always did. My parents spoke in practical sentences. The radio played softly in the background. Breakfast was eaten without ceremony. No one asked where I had been. No one noticed how I walked a little slower. The world hadn't shifted, even though I felt like something fundamental had broken.

Sunday arrived without ceremony.

Church bells rang in the distance that morning, faint but unmistakable. Normally, I would have been pulling on a shirt by now, checking my watch, rushing out the door. Instead, I stayed in bed and listened to the bells fade.

It felt like crossing an invisible line.

By late afternoon, restlessness set in. I paced the living room, then my room, then back again. The walls felt closer than usual. I thought about calling Trish, rehearsed what I might say, then imagined her voice on the other end—hesitant, guarded—and put the receiver back down.

That was when it hit me: I was afraid again. This time, fear had consequences.

Not the fear of being bullied. That was gone. This was different. This was the fear of exposure. Of having everything collapse at once—church, school, family, affiliations—stacked too neatly to survive the truth.

I realised then that power didn't always feel powerful. Sometimes it felt like waiting for a knock on the door. I didn't know yet that the knock was coming.

Only that something had already begun to close in. There would be no quiet way out.

***

PART III

25 - ACTIVATION

A phone call interrupted me as I was creating another mixtape. Some evenings, for no particular reason, to relieve some boredom, I would take some vinyls out and create mixtapes. I was learning how to DJ from Victor—so I would practice putting some songs that had similar beats together into a cassette tape and listen to it on the way to school the following day. I was halfway through recording when I heard the phone ring.

It was Victor on the phone. He didn't usually call that time of day. Something must be up.

"There is going to be an incident tonight at Six Mile," he said in almost a hushed, heightened voice.

"9.30. P.M. Make sure you're there," as he hung up quickly.

It was an activation. I froze a little and started to get nervous. Usually, when there was a call like this, it was shortly after I came home from school. It was usually between students from rival gangs.

But this time it was different. The call came after dinner. I was guessing that it was between two adults or older kids.

I was wondering what kind of excuse I would make in order for me to go out at that hour at night that needed a bit more time.

"I'm going to Victor's house to pick up some study notes for tomorrow."

It was a reasonably good excuse. Victor lived outside my neighborhood and needed a bus ride. Accounting for an hour of chit-chat before coming home, that would give me a solid two hours to do whatever Victor and the rest wanted to do. Perfect.

I made my way to Six Mile from my home. The route was half a mile, along a wide and long open drain that ran along the road. It was low tide that night and the drain was empty. The smell of the drain permeated through the night air. There was little light along the way, except a lamp-post or two, which made the walk to Six Mile especially unnerving and uncomfortable. My feet were a little lighter and faster as I found my way towards the dim light of the market.

Upon reaching the market, I made my way across the entrance, through empty stalls and wet floors, finally to the opening where I saw a small gathering of people. The seniors that I recognised were sitting around tables. But this time, not drinking anything. They had empty beer bottles on the table and sat on stools, a slight distance from the table than normal. The atmosphere was tense. I scanned across the meeting place and found Victor and the rest and joined them.

"Hey, what's going on?" I asked the guys, almost in a whisper.

"When something happens, you strike the bottle on the edge of the table like this. Don't sit too close or it's gonna be hard to stand up," said Victor, holding a beer bottle at the neck and gesturing how to cleanly strike the base of the bottle.

As we looked across, we noticed that we didn't recognise some groups of people. The rival gang was also there. That made us feel uneasy. They looked rougher and bigger than us.

I was thinking to myself, "Tonight's not gonna end well."

Seniors and seniors met rivals at a table. They talked in low voices and gestured to each other. They were discussing terms, agreeing on how they would settle their differences and negotiate terms.

At the end of the discussion, an elder nodded and two older kids, maybe 18 or 19 stood up and went to the centre of the meeting place. One of them I recognised from my school and the other was unfamiliar to me. After a gesture was made from the elder, with no weapons, they started to hit each other. Everyone else sat in their place.

I could hear curse words in Chinese dialect as the two pounded each other with their fists—kicking and screaming.

The hair behind my head rose. I breathed heavily and my heart raced, pounding loudly. We were waiting for another signal from the elders. But none came. I gripped the table as I watched the two guys fight.

The one I recognised fell on the floor and the other guy kicked him hard in the stomach a few times. It was all over now and he immediately took his shirt off, exposing his bare torso, and ran quickly out of the market. Others followed him. There was no retaliation—just a dispersion of the gathering.

We immediately got off our seats, ran out of the market and quickly disappeared into the darkness of the path along the drain. It was so dark we couldn't tell who was who. Apparently, it's harder to identify someone by what he was wearing if he had taken his shirt off.

As soon as my head hit my pillow that night, I fell asleep quickly. I was exhausted. I didn't feel the guilt that I used to feel for getting involved in an incident like that. I was numb to it all. I woke up in the morning and felt nothing. I quickly dressed and went to school.

This was the way things were. When we were activated, we would respond to the call. At this point,

I was never part of a challenge. Just backup. Most of the time, the challenger was the one that was involved. If there was a payoff, the matter was resolved quietly. Otherwise, a fight ensued.

A couple of weeks later, I saw the same guy that got hit badly in school. He had a crutch and was limping to class. He had broken ribs and a sprained ankle from the fall. I heard him saying, "You should have seen the other guy."

I told myself, "Well, that wasn't what I saw."

***

26 - WHAT WASN'T SAID

THOUGHTS of the stairwell incident sank in and faded after a few weeks. I wanted to forget it, but every now and then, it replayed itself anyway—uninvited, relentless.

I think Michael heard about the incident from different sources at church, but decided to give me space and didn't want to talk to me about it. He understood me well enough to leave me alone and didn't call. Besides, he didn't know what to say. Most times, we talked about everything except our own affairs and feelings. It wasn't something guys our age talked about. If things went bad, we would just suck it up.

Victor probably heard about it too, through school. Trent would have been boasting about it to his club friends. I suppose Victor would have felt some rage when one in his gang was assaulted, but he decided it was not worth pursuing. I wasn't hurt, and I didn't want to escalate anything with

Trent. It was a fight over a girl, and that was the last thing he wanted involvement with according to their rule book. We didn't fight over girls. Period.

I never called Trish to apologize for ruining her party either. I was embarrassed, but I was also angry at her for revealing what I had said to an outsider. I expected what we said to be kept between us. I felt betrayed. I didn't expect her to be close to Trent—not in the way that we were close.

It was a deafening silence between the four of us. Nothing could have been said to improve things. There was a mood of emptiness inside me, as if something had swallowed all my emotions and left me hollow. For once, music didn't play in my head. Not a single song. Silence became the only thing that felt safe.

Not long after, on Monday at school, my form-teacher pulled me out and told me to report to the Principal's office. My chest tightened and I broke into a cold sweat. Have I been found out? My mind raced through different incidents from the past, and I couldn't think of a single thing I had done in school that broke the rules.

I followed my form-teacher down the stairs, and it felt like a walk of shame. As I passed the hallways, kids from each class peered out of their windows and stared at me. The feeling was excruciating. My feet wobbled. I believed I was going to have to pick a cane for my punishment. If it came to that, I was going for medium, I told myself. The thin cane would tear into my buttocks and the large one would leave me unable to sit for days.

"So I know you got into a fight," the Principal boomed in an intimidating, commanding voice.

The moment those words rang out, my heart exploded in my chest. My legs felt like jelly and tears started streaming down my face. He knew the truth and he was coming for blood. He was the most feared person on the planet. He wasn't large —almost my height—but with fierce eyebrows and a greying, pulled-back hairline, he made me feel very small. He might as well have been a fire-spewing dragon. I froze in horror. Could this be about the five guys we had beaten up opposite the school?

"The parents of a girl at Catechism reported an incident and said that you were involved."

He demanded details, but I wouldn't give any. It was Trish's parents who had filed the complaint.

"I'm going to call your parents."

My dad rushed down to school. When he opened the General Office door, our eyes did not meet. I embarrassed him. Calling the General Office was no trivial matter. In those days, we didn't have Parent-Teacher Conferences or discussions about student welfare and development. It was a no news is good news policy.

He met with the Principal behind closed doors while I sat outside, not knowing what was happening. From the corridor, I could hear strained voices, but nothing pieced together except the words "fight," "birthday," and "another school." I could infer they were talking about Trish's birthday incident. An investigation was underway—phone calls were made, questions asked, facts clarified. All this while, I stared at the ceiling of the General Office, watched the ceiling fan and replayed the incident over and over again as beads of sweat dripped from my head.

After three hours, my dad came out. His face was red. He looked flustered.

"Let's go," he said firmly, pulling me toward our family car.

He didn't speak as he drove home. I was terrified. I kept glancing in his direction but received no validation, no judgment—just silence. When we got home, all he did was ask me to have lunch, which he brought for me, reminded me to have dinner out, and then went back to the shop. It was a busy time and this was the last thing he needed.

I was left alone to process what had just transpired. I was numb the entire day. I didn't speak, sleep, or turn on the music. There was an uncomfortable silence in my home and my mind. Yet again, I suffered in silence.

That evening, my parents came home and my

dad found me in my room. He had visibly calmed down.

"Have you eaten?" he asked.

I was asked to have dinner out since they were working late.

"No, I'm not hungry," I said softly.

His voice broke something in me, and I started to cry.

"So the situation is like this," he said.

"The Principal wanted to expel you for being involved in a gang-related fight. But after investigating further, no gangs were involved and you did not fight back. You were attacked. Why didn't you tell me about this?"

"It was nothing. Some stupid party I went to," I tried to explain, but he cut me off.

"If it wasn't for this girl who stood up for you, you would have been expelled for sure," he said.

***

27 - QUIET INTERVENTION

"SHE said she saw everything and asked her parents not to complain to the school," my dad continued.

"But they did anyway."

It was then that I realised Trish had stood up for me. She regretted sharing our conversation with Trent. While she tried to make the best of a bad situation, her parents wanted justice.

After everything we had been through, I guess she still cared about me and protected me.

I didn't know what to feel—only that I was overwhelmed.

"I'll only tell you once. If you go down this path, you will end up nowhere. If you can study, then study," my dad said firmly.

"Otherwise, go learn a trade and be useful."

Those words hit me hard. But the truth of his

words rang loudly.

I saw my father in a completely different light that day. All these years, I had the wrong impression of him. I saw very little of him growing up. He spoke very little, especially to me. I figured he cared less since my parents were always busy. He was a silent figure in my life. I didn't see him as a provider or a protector—someone who would keep me safe. I only remembered him at his most vulnerable point, when he lost his job and his sense of purpose. I had lost respect for him. Naively, I thought he had failed at work and been fired.

I had expected him to be furious about what happened and dreaded his involvement with the school, his intrusion into my life and my friends. This was the part of my life I kept hidden from my family. I never brought friends home or spoke about them. Deliberately opaque about my activities in school and after school, I also assumed he wouldn't want to hear my version of the incident and would simply impose punishment.

Most of the time, I wasn't close to him and couldn't read his mind. To me, he was a figure of fear. In those days, most fathers were distant, uninvolved, and ruled with a heavy hand. But he went in a completely different direction and caught me by surprise.

The school principal had been aggressive and presumptuous about the entire incident. But at my father's insistence, he called the parents again to clarify matters, and Trish stepped in with her version of the story. No further names were divulged.

"Two wrongs don't make a right," my dad said.

He argued that what happened to me did not warrant expulsion. The other boys involved should be treated separately by their own school. But he wanted proper punishment for me.

Still, I wasn't entirely blameless. I had put myself in that situation. I had gone to the party. I was involved in a fight. I would be disciplined—but it wouldn't go on record like an expulsion would.

That day, my view of my father changed. His quiet, masterful handling of the situation had diffused it. He protected me in a way I had never imagined. He also saved face for the principal, who had been pushing for a more severe reprimand even though I was the victim.

My fear of my father turned into deep respect.

My dad explained that he and the principal were former schoolmates, and he eventually negotiated for me to attend detention classes after school for two weeks. There, I would receive extra lessons. I was grounded and not allowed out of the house after school, and I had to call him from home every day. It was a healthy compromise. Everyone got what they wanted.

He reached into his pocket and pulled out an

envelope with a letter inside. The envelope had already been opened.

"You should avoid all these gangs and have more friends like this," he said, handing it to me.

His face softened.

"Dear Alan,

I know you haven't been at church lately and we miss having you around. I'm just saying hello and wishing you all the best for the mid-year exams.

Best of luck.

— Michael"

It had been sent weeks earlier, before Trish's birthday party. My dad had been suspicious of how much time I spent away from home. When the letter arrived in our mailbox, he opened it to see who I had been mixing with. He was concerned about the change in my behaviour, but he didn't react immediately. He wanted to observe, to see where things would land.

It wasn't indecision—it was quiet intervention.

My dual life almost collapsed that day. I had nearly been exposed. I realised that if I had used my gang affiliations to deal with Trent, I would have been expelled for sure. The outcome would have been very different. And perhaps by luck alone, doing nothing had saved me. My father showed me power that day—a very different kind of power.

The familiar five-note jingle and rhythmic beat started playing in my head again, louder than ever before.

"There's a room where the light won't find you,

Holding hands while the walls come tumbling down

When they do, I'll be right behind you."

My hand was held as my walls crumbled. And when they did, my dad was right behind me, along with Trish.

***

28 - DOING NOTHING WASN'T NEUTRAL

DETENTION in May was every day after school, for two hours each day, over two weeks. Since school finished at 1 P.M., I was allowed 30 minutes for lunch, followed by 90 minutes of extra lessons. It also doubled as revision classes, and I had the chance to be coached one-on-one by subject teachers as mid-term exams approached. The structure of detention strangely calmed me. The hum of the fans, the fluorescent lights, and the routine of studying did exactly that.

"What if this was a better way out?" I thought.

I sat for the exams and didn't think too much about them afterward.

I didn't call Trish after detention. I didn't want to resolve anything. I wanted a clean break from the incident. Putting distance between us was my way of letting time do the work. I wouldn't have known what to say anyway. I also stayed away from church. Between the humiliation I had experienced and the detention that followed, there would have been plenty of rumours circulating, and it felt safer to leave things as they were.

Exam results were released in the last week of May, before we broke for the mid-year school holidays. I had put in more effort than usual but didn't expect much in return. There was a small improvement in my results and class ranking. I had moved fifteen places from near the bottom to the middle of the class, with mostly Bs. There was nothing to celebrate. I was tired, but I knew I had to put in much more work if I truly wanted better results.

The mid-year school holidays went by quickly and without incident. I spent most of it staying out of trouble and occasionally hanging out with Victor again, helping him spin records at various functions. I attended only one society meeting that month. I wanted to show visibility and presence, but there weren't any unresolved issues that required gang-related intervention. At the same time, I was gradually distancing myself from it.

As quickly as the holidays ended, we were back at the Community Centre, hanging out more often. There was a group we grew close to from another school. They were rougher than usual and not good at studies. But I made friends with them easily because they felt real. Very real.

Every day, they showed up, studied a little, but mostly filled their time playing basketball. They would spend hours on the basketball court, just throwing hoops, laughing and fooling around. Nothing seemed to bother them.

One day, out of the blue, one of them—Meng—came to us asking for help. They had been challenged by another group over a staring incident. They wanted our help to make up the numbers and didn't think it would result in a fight. They didn't ask where we were from or who we knew. They didn't look dangerous. They just assumed we'd stand there with them.

So we agreed to help. Our plan was to talk things through openly and hopefully reach a no-contest resolution. We didn't think it was risky. A date was set for the end of the week to meet at the Community Centre after dark.

On the day of the meeting, I made an excuse to my parents that I was staying over at Victor's place to study. A partial truth. I was planning to stay over, but not to study—it was to attend the challenge and then spend the night at his house.

As I was preparing to leave, the phone rang.

“` Lan,” a familiar voice said. It was Trish.

“I need to speak to you in person,” she said. Her voice was trembling, and I sensed urgency. She had never spoken to me before like this.

"I'm about to go out. Can we talk this weekend at church?" I said, with only Meng and the guys on my mind.

"Don't go. Something bad will happen. It's Trent. He's involved with your friends from the Community Centre, and he's bringing people from outside."

I panicked.

"How did she know what was going on?" I thought.

I had always kept this part of my life from her and never spoke about it.

"I overheard Trent bragging about it. He's setting up a trap. Please don't go," she pleaded.

Putting the phone down, I immediately started calling Victor and the others, but they had already left early to stake out the Community Centre. This was really bad. I left a terse message on Victor's answering machine.

"Call me back right away," I said and bolted out.

The only way to reach them was by bus. I had planned to leave an hour later but this was urgent. I ran to the bus stop and waited for the next one, sweating as fear and anxiety raced through me.

Then the unexpected happened. Along the way, traffic ground to a halt. A car had broken down in the middle of the road.

"Of all places, he had to break down on his road, at this time," complained the passenger next to me.

I could only nod nervously.

My uneasiness grew—please, please go faster.

After what seemed like an eternity, I watched the car being secured to a tow truck and the road finally started to clear. As the bus slowly passed the stalled car, I could see the traffic warden waving the vehicles onward one by one with a red baton. The bus picked up speed, but dread had already settled in. I wondered if it was too late.

When I arrived fifteen or twenty minutes late, my heart sank. Bystanders had formed a loose perimeter around the basketball court where the meeting was supposed to have taken place. The scene worried me as I went closer.

The group we were supposed to back up was already on the ground, injured and crying softly. Meng was seriously injured, slumped in a small pool of blood. Victor and the others were nowhere to be seen. There were distant sirens from police cars and ambulances as they raced toward the scene.

"What happened?" I asked myself as my thoughts raced.

My heart pounded as I tried to make sense of it. Panicking, I quietly slipped away, my pace quickening as I moved away from the scene and disappeared. I was afraid.

I must have wandered the neighbourhood for over an hour before finally arriving at Victor's home.

He shot me a look.

"Where were you?"

I explained that there was an accident along the way and I couldn't get there earlier. Besides, the meeting was supposed to be later.

"What were you guys doing there so early?" I shot back.

"Meng's badly hit. The police and ambulance were called, so we all split," he said matter-of-factly.

"I think Trent was involved," I said, explaining what I saw when I arrived.

I realised he was taking revenge for being expelled from school. His real target was *me*.

He got to Meng to get to me.

Victor had a deep cut on his arm, probably from being slashed as he fled.

"Yeah, he was. We were ambushed. Guys came out of vans with knives and poles. They hit Meng and the others first. We just ran wherever we could."

He was still shaking.

That was when I understood something I hadn't before. Doing nothing wasn't neutral.

Everybody Wants To Survive the Night.

***

29 - EVERYTHING FALLS APART

WHEN Trish realised her parents were taking action over what happened on her birthday, fear settled into her chest and refused to leave. She tried to normalize it by saying that it was nothing and kids in the neighbourhood fight like that all the time.

But the real fear was that both people that were in her life right now—her *brother* from church and her partner captain from the district competition would be impacted. She would have to choose her allegiance and at this point, emotionally, she didn't want to be rational. She didn't want justice. She wanted time—time to pass, to blur, to let things return to how they were before anyone had names for what happened.

But her parents were adamant that something had to be done.

"If kids were not taught a lesson in life, they would go on and cause other problems later," declared her father.

Her father was a principled man and always tried to do the right thing. Trish inherited these principles, but now her sense of panic was stronger.

She pleaded and pleaded, but her father went ahead anyway, placing a call to my school and then to Trent's school, speaking to the respective principals and filing his complaint. He made it clear that if the school did not propose a course of action that he was satisfied with, he would go to the police and that was an outcome that no one wanted. He acted with little emotion—he wanted things to be done.

Fearful that day, she went to school, not knowing what transpired between the principals and her parents in the morning. She came home early that afternoon to find her dad on the phone.

Her dad looked up and said, "She's here, I'll give the phone to her and she can explain what she saw."

Not knowing the context of what was going on, she was handed her father's phone receiver. On the other end was a deep but loud voice. It was the principal of her *brother's* school and wanted to know what had happened. Her throat tightened as she spoke. Each sentence felt like a door closing behind her.

Trish gave her account of the events as truthfully as she could remember. She added that her *brother* was the victim and was attacked by the others.

"I saw everything—he was attacked," she told the voice on the phone, in between sobs.

She knew that by saying that, there would be consequences. At that time, she only wanted to say what was in her heart, that she had to protect the innocent and let the chips fall as they did. She handed the phone back to her father, who spoke briefly and then hung up.

A week passed and life seemed to return to normal. She went to school and came home early each time. She wanted to be available to her parents, but more so, she was emotionally tired and didn't want to hang around school. Her circle of friends were closing in on her and were wearing her down with the constant questions about what her parents did and what not. She just wanted to be left alone. No phone calls, no updates from her. Just silence.

When the day of the weekly joint practice came, she wanted to skip, but decided it was too risky. The competition was closing and it was the last push. So she went but was prepared to face more questioning from her peers. She would also have to face Trent, who probably was questioned by his school principal as well. Putting on a brave face, she entered the school and went straight to the club's home room.

Instead, the two teachers-in-charge from both schools were there talking and everyone had been asked to leave.

“Tricia, please join us,” her teacher-in-charge said, as she walked in.

She sat next to both teachers, a little anxious about things. Now news would have spread to the teachers and she would, yet again, have to explain the situation to them. She held her own hands very tightly and placed them under the table, nervous about what was about to happen.

“Trent has been expelled from school, in case you didn’t know,” her teacher-in-charge said and paused thoughtfully, allowing the news to sink in.

“This was related to the incident at your home, which we believe you witnessed,” she continued.

She stopped hearing the rest. The room felt smaller, airless. The school has a zero tolerance policy for violence in or out of school and as such, with him being primarily responsible for the incident, he was expelled.

“Now, you probably have a lot of questions about what happens to the district competition, and so on,” said her teacher and paused.

“Both of us have decided to withdraw our participation in this year’s competition,” she gestured to the other teacher.

“With Trent gone, I don’t think we can continue,” she said and shook her head.

Trish felt like she was struck with a rock. Her

entire world came crashing now on her. The competition was everything to her. They had been preparing for months and now, they wouldn't have a chance to compete. It was one of the hardest decisions that she had to swallow in her young life.

She pleaded with the teachers and suggested replacements from the boy's side, but the teachers have already made up their minds. They have already withdrawn this morning, and were only there to make sure everyone knew about the decision.

She went home devastated, went straight to her room and didn't come out for dinner. Thoughts about her being responsible for the escalation came back and flooded her mind.

"Did I say something wrong?" she asked herself.

She later learned that her *brother* was punished by two weeks of detention. Trent's group of boys had similar punishments of detention, but Trent, as the mastermind, was not let off leniently. He had planned the attack, convinced his friends to participate and used her birthday party as the stage.

One night, the phone rang and Trish picked up the phone. It was Trent. He sounded desperate and wounded. His pride was hurt and he spoke with much resentment in that voice. Initially he asked about her and the competition, and circled around what was said to the principal, etc. He was clearly fishing for information, but she was guarded and wouldn't give up too much except the known facts.

"I'm really *sorry* about what happened. I'm going to make things right by apologising to your *brother* directly," he said, sounding contrite.

He wanted to know where he was after school.

She thought he really sounded genuine about what he wanted to do to make amends. Perhaps he was a good guy after all, she told herself. This was all a misunderstanding.

But she hesitated for a minute. She shouldn't say anything. She knew that. But the silence pressed on her.

"He's been going to the Study Club at the Community Centre, with this group of guys—Meng and Victor?" she said finally.

"I heard Victor has secret society affiliations," Trent said.

Her chest tightening again, from the already tense conversation. She wasn't sure where this was going. But realising who her *brother* was mixing up with spelt caution. Then almost in a 180 degree turn in terms of tone and intention, Trent blurted out.

"I'll show those guys who have real affiliations. I'm going to finish him off." He hung up.

Trish was shocked at his reaction. Not that she didn't expect that this would not happen. But at that rate the conversation turned sour.

In the days that followed, reaching out to her St. John's network, she learnt what Trent had already set in motion. He had approached Meng, fabricated a challenge and was going to use outsiders to ambush the group. He wanted revenge—and he wanted someone else to bleed for it.

She had seen what Trent was capable of and this time, she had to be quick, and prevent it or someone was going to get hurt again. This time, she didn't just feel it. She knew it.

***

30 - LEADERSHIP WITHOUT EXPOSURE

NEWS of the stairwell incident reached Victor within days. It always did. Incidents like that had a way of travelling quietly through overlapping circles—through classmates, bus routes, whispered conversations after school—not as complete stories, but as fragments that carried enough weight to signal that something had shifted.

By the group's logic, an attack on one member was, in principle, an attack on all. That was the understanding they had adopted early on, not as a rule written down anywhere, but as an expectation that shaped how they moved together in public and how they responded when one of them was threatened.

But there was another rule, just as firmly held, and more often invoked when things became complicated.

"No fights over girls. That's the rule," he said.

It was considered undignified, impulsive, and ultimately pointless in disputes over girls. Fighting over a girl did not demonstrate strength or loyalty; it invited attention, created confusion, and blurred responsibility in ways that were difficult to control. Victor had agreed with this rule from the beginning, and now he found himself leaning on it without hesitation.

He chose not to act.

This time, he did not refer the matter upward to his seniors. He had reached a point where he understood when escalation was unnecessary and when it was, in fact, a liability. As a minor senior, he had been given a degree of discretion, and with it, the responsibility to decide which incidents mattered and which were better left unresolved. What he decided here would stand, and he was comfortable with that.

There were also rumours circulating—that Trent had connections elsewhere, that he was not acting alone, that he had been seen associating with people Victor recognised but preferred to keep his distance from. Victor told himself that his reluctance to get involved was not fear, but judgment. Knowing when not to intervene, he believed, was a form of discipline, and discipline was what separated leaders from followers.

Over time, Victor had learned how conflicts were

meant to unfold. When things reached seniors, things slowed. Names were exchanged, grievances formalised, apologies negotiated. But most situations never rose to that level. Minor disputes could be handled quietly. Challenges could be defused. More often than not, money changed hands and the matter ended there.

"If money can solve the problem, it's not a problem," he famously said.

Victor always preferred that outcome.

Violence, on the other hand, created complications. It attracted attention, invited retaliation, and left behind consequences that were difficult to predict. And when violence was unavoidable, it was better if it did not lead directly back to you.

From a young age, Victor had learned that power was most effective when exercised from a distance. He was rarely the first to speak and almost never the one to step forward. He let others raise their voices, take positions, and assume risks. He stayed close enough to guide the outcome, but far enough away to avoid visibility. If something went wrong, it was never his decision—only his presence.

That distance protected him.

It also meant that when situations escalated beyond what he anticipated, they did so without him at the centre of it.

Victor did not follow up on Trent. He did not warn anyone. He did not signal retaliation or protection. He told himself that this was neutrality—that by stepping back, he was allowing the situation to dissolve on its own.

But he understood the streets well enough to know that unresolved anger rarely disappeared. It merely shifted, waiting for the right moment, the right place, and the right group of people who would absorb the consequences.

Others would take the risks and Victor would retain the influence.

His inaction put Meng in the hospital.

***

31 - ACTING ON YOUR BEST BEHAVIOUR

MENG spent the next two weeks in hospital. He was badly hurt. He had been the first to be attacked when it happened and had protected the rest of the guys while they scattered. Two broken ribs, slashes on his hands and legs. They were unarmed, unlike the attackers. We couldn't visit him for fear of being associated with the incident. Police had interviewed him several times but he didn't give anyone up. There was a street code—no names, no statements, no questions. Silence was loyalty.

I told myself I was lucky. Someone else had paid for that luck. I hadn't been there when it happened. I wasn't hurt. Again. But the truth was harder to sit. I hadn't thrown a punch. I had even tried to warn them. Still, someone bled on the ground. Doing nothing hadn't kept anyone safe. This thought lingered on me for a long while and ate me up inside. I didn't think about revenge, loyalty, or fear. I thought about school. About exams. About disappearing.

This wasn't a life I could manage. It was one I had to leave—or it would decide for me.

The attack was covered in the local afternoon newspaper, but it was on the second page and only a footnote. It was enough to send us underground. Victor, the rest and I didn't contact each other. We minimised interaction and stayed out of sight. We feared that the police would be looking for suspects and we couldn't risk being noticed. The Community Centre did not have security cameras, and there was no video footage of the incident. And because it was at night, it had already closed for the day, and there were no witnesses. Still, we couldn't risk anything.

After Meng was discharged, we arranged to meet at the nearby playground at night. We were really concerned for him—his physical wellbeing and how he was holding up. He came and tried to smile as best as he could. But when he saw us, he broke and cried. In between sobs, he told us his version of the story. We stood close and put our hands on his shoulder. Because they were unarmed, the police were looking for the perpetrators of the attack instead. Meng wasn't off the hook—he still had to assist with investigations—but he had protected everyone else.

He told us to stay away for now. To keep our heads down. To be on our best behaviour.

"No more challenges," he said. "No stupid moves."

He was a hero to us. He acted as a big brother, protected the others and took the blows. We all cried with him, apologised that we couldn't protect him. We were all teenagers, learning to be adults, but wept like young children.

Victor suddenly turned on me. For the first time, I saw how easily power turned inward.

"Why didn't you come?" he said, accusing me of chickening out.

I tried to explain the traffic accident along the way and how I was delayed but he wouldn't have it. He became increasingly aggressive as I told my version of the story. I tried to warn them and left a message on his answering machine but it was too late. He had been carrying it for days and wanted someone to blame. I countered that the last time I was attacked by Trent, he chose to do nothing. Which was worse? Inaction or coming late? How would coming any earlier change things?

"Stop!" Meng shouted and broke the escalating situation, cringing a little, his hands holding his broken ribs.

"Vic, you ran like everyone else. Should we also call you a coward?" Meng shot. The temperature went down immediately.

That was the end of it. No more words were said and we quietly parted ways.

That was the last time I ever saw Meng, Victor, or the rest.

"Most of freedom and of pleasure. Nothing ever lasts for ever," the song rang in my mind.

I never asked where Victor went after that or looked him up. I lost respect for him. I suspect he had already moved on long before the rest of us realised there was nothing left to stay for.

It took me years to understand that to him, people were never anchors—they were leverage. When the leverage ran out, so did he.

What the rest of us saw that night was simple. Victor wanted power, but only if it came without cost to him. Meng never asked for it. He earned it by standing in front, by protecting his friends—staying when others ran, by taking the consequences into his own body.

To me, Victor was *really* just another spoiled rich kid, and Meng was the real deal.

That was the difference.

***

32 - WHEN THE RAIN PASSED

AFTER the incident at the Community Centre, I laid low and stayed home most days after school. To fill my time, on some occasions, I would help out at the shop. I didn't stay all day. I would usually go around closing time. I took the bus to town, which took almost an hour. The journey started from the Six Mile market, meandered through traffic, stopping at endless traffic lights before finally arriving in town. On the bus, I would daydream. My mind wandered aimlessly, weaving through recent incidents, friends I had met, and the two people who remained closest to me—Trish and Michael. Those years had been traumatic, and more than anything, I just wanted to fade away.

I thought about why things had turned for the worse but found no clear answers. Instead, I remembered feeling trapped and more alone than ever. My inaction and indecision had served me well up to that point. But I also knew it was plain luck that I hadn't been hurt, expelled from school, or worse, arrested. I thought about church life and the society, how different yet similar they were. Both had rules, people, places. Both were well-organised, with social norms and hierarchy. Where they diverged was in their outcomes and objectives. One ruled through fear and violence; the other through herd mentality and a shared sense of morality. To me, they didn't sound all that different. I was searching for belonging, but neither gave it to me. Both had dislodged me, and I couldn't find solace or happiness in either. I felt worn down by the effort of wanting the right thing.

When I reached the shop, I helped count the cash, close the register, tidy up, and pull down the shutters with my dad. We would then go for dinner together. My brothers avoided the shop and were never involved. As far as I could remember, I had never seen them there. I wasn't thrilled about it either, but having dinner earlier was a fair trade. It also broke the monotony of my days and eased the uneasiness that followed me everywhere.

I never told my dad about detention. I was expected to accept punishment and endure it. By then, it felt like a distant memory, and I was eager to move past it with him. Besides, what had happened at the Community Centre was far worse. Someone had been hurt, really bad. If he ever found out, I was sure I would have been in serious trouble—perhaps even sent to a boys' home. I knew that if I had gone on much longer, things would only have worsened.

One night, as we were closing the shop, my dad watched me for a long moment before speaking. I expected a lecture—a reminder to focus, or a reprimand for the way I had been drifting.

Instead, he said quietly, "Things must be tough for you these few years."

He paused. The shutters rattled as we pulled them down, filling a silence he didn't rush to break.

"When something goes bad, it's not the end of the world. It cannot rain all the time, and it can't be sunny all the time."

It was the most I had ever heard him say in all the years I'd known him. He told me about his job, and how heartbroken he had been when he was forced to let go of his colleagues because the company was failing.

"We had a good run. But when the recession hit, we lost everything."

His colleagues had families, daily expenses, and lives to lead. He was responsible for them, yet powerless to stop the company from closing. The CEO had gone bankrupt. Debts piled up. My dad had no choice but to shut everything down. Being who he was, he didn't complain or ask for severance. He knew he would have to lay himself off in the end. He did it because it was his job.

He had to travel to the overseas branches to deliver the bad news and close those businesses. When it was all done, he came home and barely spoke for days. It took a toll on him. He kept himself busy with small repairs around the house, trying to quiet his thoughts. He tried to return to the same industry, but opportunities at his level had dried up. It was raining hard in his life.

Unexpectedly, he set aside his pride and went to help my mother at the shop. He wanted to be useful. He chose to act, changing his circumstances without knowing where it would lead.

"What's the worst that could happen?" he said. "We fail, and then we start again."

He believed deeply that life came in seasons—ups and downs—and that you did what you could with what you were given. Eventually, the rain passed. Business picked up after the worst of the recession, and things gradually improved. We were no longer underwater.

That night, he passed something on to me that I still carry today. As the shutters rattled and slammed shut, the sound echoed down the empty corridor. I stood beside him, feeling the weight settle—not on the ground, but on me.

And for the first time, I didn't resist it.

***

33 - LEARNING TO STAY

"THERE is some method in the madness," Michael said as he explained his approach to studying.

"You work with the end in mind," he added confidently.

He wasn't the top student in his class, but he hovered around the top ten each year. That was enough for me. I valued his input because, unlike most people, he made progress without making noise about it.

Together, we created a daily work schedule. I moaned at the amount of work laid out before me. I had to pull every effort to improve my grades by the end of the year. I was in a different stream from Michael, which meant we couldn't study together. We shared some common subjects, but those were never my problem areas. He wasn't a taskmaster either. He checked in casually once in a while, but the work itself was mine to do.

Studying did not come naturally to me. I didn't turn in homework, I daydreamed in class, and I had the attention span of a goldfish. I couldn't sit still or focus for long. The first thing I realised I had to fix was my impatience—the inability to stay with something when it became uncomfortable.

To do that, I had to remove distractions. Each afternoon after school, I retreated to my room. The silence there was deafening, so I filled it with music. That proved to be a mistake. Every new song pulled me off my books. I sang along without thinking, counted beats, drifted back into rhythms I knew too well. Eventually, I changed the music to instrumental pieces. Strangely, that worked. I still noticed the tempo, still counted beats per minute out of habit, but the pull was weaker. I could sit longer. I could stay.

Invitations to functions still came occasionally. I turned them down. After missing enough of them, the invitations stopped. It wasn't fun to be around me anymore.

My attention span was still short. Reading textbooks felt painful and slow. Michael suggested I practise reading long-form text instead. He said it might help build stamina. I was doubtful, but I trusted him. I started with short stories and essays, partly to improve my writing. Over time, I moved on to short novels and re-read literature texts from earlier years. Gradually, I found I could retain information better. Not easily, but consistently.

Every piece of homework assigned had to be completed and handed in. This was the hardest part of the change. I hadn't turned in homework regularly since Secondary One. I had ignored it long enough that my teachers stopped expecting anything from me. When I started submitting work again, they were surprised. Then they began marking it seriously. They encouraged me. Slowly, I gained enough confidence to approach them with questions. They helped readily, as if they had been waiting for me to ask.

Of all the subjects, Math was my weakest. I had to do double time on every topic. At this point, every paper would be a marginal pass—C. It got me worried. Every homework was filled with corrections. I worked late into the night, scratching my head, trying to figure out how to solve problems that seemed easy for everyone. That's when I turned to my form-teacher for help after school, who was very patient with me. She would quietly sit by me and shake her head—"No, not like that," she would say and correct me.

I prepared for the exams in earnest. Michael helped me work out revision schedules that balanced content review with past-year papers. It was only then that I realised how weak my foundation was. At first, I memorised answers blindly. Over time, understanding followed. Not all at once, but enough to keep going.

One evening, the thought crossed my mind: Had I turned into a nerd?

I barely recognised myself. I stayed home more. I spoke less. The quiet gave me space to take stock of my life. Everything I had done in the past few years, I was determined to undo—not dramatically, but deliberately.

Sometimes I thought about Trish. The thoughts lingered briefly, then passed. I missed her and wanted to reconnect, but I didn't trust myself to do it properly. So I gave it time. Time, I believed, could absorb damage that words could not. I couldn't imagine what she had gone through after everything fell apart. I was certain only of one thing: I wasn't ready to reach out.

By the 1986 final exams, I had made some progress. My form-teacher noticed. She had been tracking my work quietly. When the results were released, she looked at me and said, almost in jest, "Well, guess who is the most improved student among us?" I had reached the top ten in class, and I felt that I could push for a better result next time.

I took that as encouragement—not because I had arrived anywhere, but because I had finally begun to stay.

***

34 - WHAT POWER COSTS

BY Christmas of 1986, I stopped contact with Victor and the guys completely. The fight was too traumatic for us all, and that was when the group decided to split up. We had not spoken to each other. Fear of the police, shock at how quickly violence arrived, and the instinct to flee drove the group apart inevitably.

Trish was nowhere to be seen. I left a few messages on her answering machine, but they went unreturned.

"Hey, you disappeared—call me, okay?"

Everyday, I checked the answering machine but the result was always the same.

"No messages found," the robotic voice would return.

I guess she didn't want to have anything to do with either of us anymore—and I didn't blame her. I later learnt from Michael that her school had dropped out of the district competition and she mostly went home alone after school. No one from the Sunday choir had seen her either.

There were moments when I thought about trying again—saying something clearer, braver, more honest. But every version of that conversation ended the same way in my head: with silence. Whatever had passed between us had been crushed under things neither of us had asked for. Power had entered the room long before either of us understood its cost, and once it did, there was no way to return to who we had been. Some distances aren't chosen. They arrive and stay.

Sometimes, when the daily news on the radio came on, I still thought of how a building could disappear in the middle of an ordinary morning, the bravery of the rescuers and the tragedy. Lives were upended, some were lost—and yet, life kept going on anyway. That day, Trish, Michael and I saw unspeakable horror, yet couldn't help feeling helpless. As helpless as the families that were affected. That too, passed and gradually faded into history as a silent footnote.

My dad's words sank in, and I followed his advice. It wasn't explicit. It was the principles behind what he said that stayed with me.

"Otherwise, go learn a trade and be useful."

I was determined to change my circumstances. And so, I poured all my effort into my studies. The method in the madness Michael had taught me finally began to take hold.

Secondary Four was a make-or-break year. It meant sitting for the Preliminary exams by mid-year and the GCE 'O' Levels later that year. I put up a desk calendar, set milestones, and followed my study schedule closely. Studying became my way out of the neighbourhood—away from rough kids, gangs, and violence.

Michael and I kept in touch as we made our final ascent towards the Preliminary Exams. It was like climbing Mt Everest for me. I was full of aches and pains by then, but we had to push on. The end was in sight. We had reached base camp and were ready for the peak—the GCE 'O' Level exams. I was a little worried going into the exams with my Math abilities—I guess I couldn't be good at everything.

By the Preliminary exams, I was in the top five. For the first time, it felt possible. I scored mostly As and two Bs (Math was one of them). I remember thinking that if I could turn those Bs into As, I might get five to seven points in the final exams. Quietly, my form-teacher encouraged me. She handed me test paper after test paper to practise with everyday. I had nothing left to lose, so I went all in.

With the same rigour, both of us encouraged each other and sat for the 'O' levels exams. Sleep was scarce, fatigue set in, but we were determined to at least retain our performance or improve upon it. I had no expectations going in.

"What are the odds that I could get the same results?" I told myself.

I was going home one day after the exams and I thought I saw Trish waiting at the bus stop. I wanted to approach her, but she quickly squeezed into a bus that arrived and disappeared from sight. I reached home and decided to call her. But her home phone returned a dead tone. I lost contact after.

Whatever happened between the two of us was crushed under the weight of events that neither of us asked for. Like the mixtape that was destroyed at the stairwell, it had recorded milestones, memories and emotions of us growing up. The crushed plastic and mangled ribbon could never be recovered. The relationship between Trish and I had reached a distance that was never meant to survive. Power had entered the room long before either of us understood its cost, and once it did, there was no way to return to who we were.

As for Victor, I heard from rumours that he didn't take the 'O' levels exams and dropped out after the Preliminaries. He decided to pursue a course in being a professional DJ. Many years later, I heard that he didn't progress much in that career and ended up owning an audio store selling vinyl records. It closed shortly as CDs took the world by storm. He had lost his family's money in the process. Nothing much more was heard of him.

Because my Preliminary results were strong, I applied to a top-five junior college in a different neighbourhood. I was the only one from my school who did. I was proud of myself for even trying.

I bumped into my form-teacher on the way out of school and she asked me, "So, which JC are you going to?"

With a confident smile I told her the name of the school.

"Good lord!" she exclaimed. "Good luck to them," she quipped with a broad smile. You could see the satisfaction and pride in her eyes that day.

The following year, before the GCE 'O' Level results were released in March, I started attending school outside my neighbourhood.

Michael had decided to stay in the neighbourhood and went to a school nearby. True to his nature, he didn't want to go to a top school. There was too much pressure to do well.

I was the underdog in many ways in my new school. There were students far smarter than me, but I kept reminding myself that I had every right to be there. I struggled to keep pace, but I was loving every minute of it.

When the GCE 'O' Level results were announced, I was stunned. The principal addressed the entire school and said there were two students who had scored perfect As that year. My name was called. As I shook hands and received the school award from the principal, he made a little wink at me. I returned with a sheepish, modest smile. I had earned my way there—earned my way out of the neighbourhood—and earned a new life ahead.

I went straight to the shop that day filled with pride. I had done what I was never supposed to do. My dad was so proud. I had made his day. My parents closed the shop early that evening and we went home together.

Like every other day, we ate dinner with our heads bowed. Little was said, but everything was understood. There was no celebration, no speech. I took a deep breath and finally let it out. I looked up and met my dad's eyes. He gave a small nod and began clearing the plates.

There was one thing left unresolved. Before I left the neighbourhood for good, I needed to face it. Later that night, I made some excuse and walked alone to the Six Mile market to confront the last thing I was still afraid of. I didn't want to leave with unfinished business—not fear, not gratitude, not regret. The dreaded walk through empty stalls. Smell of dead fish and pork. The dirty, wet floor. This time, the walk was filled with resolve. I remember thinking, What's the worst that can happen? I get beaten up—and then I finally leave.

That night, only a few people were at the market. It wasn't a meeting night. Some sat at broken tables amid empty stalls, drinking warm beer. I didn't recognise anyone at first, until the senior that I knew stepped forward and stopped me. He had already passed the age when the school couldn't continue with him and dropped out. He sat me down.

"What are you doing here?" he asked.

Before I could say anything, in a deep, low voice, he said, "Aren't you someone who's good at studies?"

News of winning the school award reached his ears that day, somehow.

"Don't come back. Ever. Go and live your life."

He didn't threaten me. He didn't warn me. He dismissed me.

I had come full circle. I didn't feel brave. I didn't feel victorious. I felt finished. That was the last loose end of my adolescence. I turned and walked back through the market, past the empty stalls and wet floors that once terrified me. This time, there was no fear. I didn't look back.

As I left, the final lines of *Everybody Wants To Rule The World* played in my head again.

"So glad we've almost made it. So sad they had to fade it."

I thought the song was about power. It took me years to realise it was about what power costs—and no one wants to pay for it.

The people who had truly protected me never asked for anything in return.

***

EPILOGUE

FOUR years had passed since I left the neighbourhood to attend junior college. In that time, I had completed my GCE 'A' Levels and done well enough to qualify for a top local university.

After junior college, it was mandatory for me to serve National Service in the army for two and a half years before attending university. As a young adult, life had taken on a different rhythm—structured, demanding, and oddly grounding.

One weekend, after booking out of camp, I decided to attend Sunday Mass before going home. It was the first time I had been back since leaving the neighbourhood. Something inside me had called me to go. I showed up in my Army uniform, my hair cut short in a crew cut. I wasn't small anymore. I was medium-built now, shoulders broader, skin tanned from being outdoors.

I didn't recognise anyone during the service. I wanted to get in and out quietly. The church felt familiar yet different. The façade looked the same —nothing much had changed—but inside, the atmosphere felt softer. Less intimidating. Less intense. I sat all the way at the back, trying to remain inconspicuous. It would be easier to slip out when Mass ended.

As the service concluded, I turned and began to leave.

“`Lan?”

A familiar voice called out. I almost missed it before turning around.

Trish stood behind me.

She looked different—older, composed and fair skinned—dressed in a blouse and a dark pencil skirt. She was shorter, or had I grown taller? At first, I wasn’t sure it was her. I had to look twice. She was alone.

“Hey, Trish,” I said, almost immediately.

We shared a brief hug, then pulled away just as quickly. We hadn’t kept in touch for years. Her family had moved, though they were still in the neighbourhood, and their contact numbers had changed. Looking at her, memories from our childhood surfaced all at once. But there was also an awkward silence—uncertainty over what remained and what had quietly moved on.

“It’s my own design, it’s my own remorse,” as the song echoed in my mind.

“I didn’t know you still came,” she said.

"I don't," I said.

"I was just passing through," I added, with a faint smile.

"`Lan... I..." she lingered, as if to say something more. Our gaze locked at that moment.

"Yeah. I know." I quickly cut in, as I watched her eyes moistened.

After exchanging a few words and catching up briefly, we exchanged contact details and promised to keep in touch. Then I turned and walked away.

I rounded the corner and disappeared from her view.

***

FROM THE AUTHOR

This story is a work of fiction with some incidents and events drawn from my childhood, re-imagined to make the storyline work. Many have asked me if the characters were real. Yes—they were, but they formed from parts of different people in my life.

While the story was set in the 1980s, it is also rooted in unspeakable truths about growing up in modern Singapore—and elsewhere in the world. Research suggests that as many as one in four upper primary or secondary school students experience bullying today. While there is a zero-tolerance policy from the Ministry of Education to address this, it does not mean the problem simply disappears. It still shows up in a different form.

Whenever I read news stories about children being harassed or bullied at school, my heart goes out to them. I had a difficult time growing up in a neighbourhood school, and I recognise the fear, confusion, and isolation they may feel. It is not something that can be resolved only by vigilant teachers, but the entire ecosystem that children live in.

As a first time author, I wrote this book to shine a light on those experiences, and to invite readers to reflect on how schools have changed—and improved—over the years.

My hope is that it offers parents and readers some insight into the inner lives of teenage children, and encourages conversation, empathy, understanding, and support during the fragile years of growing up. All schools are good schools, but the underlying circumstances may be very different from one to another.

My sincere thanks to the friends and family who read the novel and offered thoughtful, constructive feedback. For that, I am deeply grateful.

Alan Yong
9 Oct 2025

ARCHIVE PHOTOS

Six Mile Market (Source: 19980005081 - 0087, National Archives)

School At The Seventh Mile (Source: Unknown)

Catholic Church At The Seventh Mile (Source: 20090000069 - 0002, National Archives)

Hotel New World Disaster (Source: 19980001166 - 0109, National Archives)

www.ingramcontent.com/pod-product-compliance
Lightning Source LLC
LaVergne TN
LVHW090514110826
845146LV00003B/854

* 9 7 8 9 8 1 9 4 5 6 3 1 4 *